I0800037

NEW MEXICO MISSION CHURCHES

NEW MEXICO MISSION CHURCHES

DONNA BLAKE BIRCHELL

THE History PRESS

Published by The History Press
Charleston, SC
www.historypress.com

Back cover: Library of Congress; *inset*: Library of Congress.

Unless otherwise noted, all images are courtesy of the author.

First published 2021

Manufactured in the United States

ISBN 9781467144933

Library of Congress Control Number: 2020951818

Notice: The information in this book is true and complete to the best of our knowledge. It is offered without guarantee on the part of the author or The History Press. The author and The History Press disclaim all liability in connection with the use of this book.

To those who endure the scourges of oppression and slavery in the name of progress while displaying conviction and grace.

Hold on to what is good
Even if it's a handful of earth
Hold on to what you believe,
Even if it's a tree that stands by itself.
Hold on to what you must do,
Even if it's a long way from here.
Hold on to your life,
Even if it's easier to let go.
Hold on to my hand,
Even if someday
I'll be gone away from you.
—Pueblo prayer

We have lived upon this land from days beyond history's records, far past any living memory, deep into the time of legend. The story of my people and the story of this place are one single story. We are always joined together.
—Pueblo elder

Our faith is drawn from the earth.
—Picuris tribal member Carl Tsosie

CONTENTS

ACKNOWLEDGEMENTS

The journey continues due to the faith of one special person—thank you, Samantha Villa, for starting this crazy ride for me.

Without the love, patience and support of my family—Jerry, Michael, Sherrie, Justin and Amanda Birchell—as well as Missy and Robert Garriott, I would be nothing. Thank you for your love and understanding and for always having my back!

To my honorary "Little Sister" Christine Florez, whose friendship and constant encouragement helped me to realize that this was all worthwhile and that it makes a difference.

Thank you to all who are fighting to preserve the rich heritage of New Mexico. Your efforts are greatly needed and appreciated.

To my extraordinary editor, Lindsey Givens, who has bravely stuck with me through several books. You do not know how much I appreciate your guidance and, of course, friendship, during these processes, which have the miraculous results of becoming a book.

INTRODUCTION

New Mexico has had a long history of turbulence and violence from its inception. Volcanic activity, some of which is still occurring under the Valles Caldera, formed the complexion of the landscape while setting the tone for the future. The lands once inhabited by many species of dinosaurs later had a human presence, which traced back to approximately 9200 BCE, when they were thought to have migrated via land bridge from Siberia in the Northern Hemisphere. The beauty and bounty of this land drew multiple cultures to the region. They developed some of the most spectacular ancient communities in what would become the United States.

The vastness of what is now New Mexico gave these cultures the ability to prosper and grow, but this vastness tended to destroy as well. Droughts, floods and extreme weather plagued the land, leading to famines, which caused many of the civilizations to leave. Several of these ancient peoples disappeared without a trace. The tough souls who endured and flourished evolved into the native people we know today.

Enduring land grabs, misunderstandings and harsh treatment, sometimes from their own people, the Native American tribes of New Mexico have had to overcome the near depletion of their cultures. A return to a higher awareness of the traditions of the ancient people has begun, as some of the pueblos have reclaimed the original names of their communities from the names given them by the Spanish explorers.

Our forty-seventh state has had much to offer, then and now. Clear turquoise skies overlay seemingly endless acres of diverse landscapes beckoning the visitor to absorb each experience. Consider this an open invitation to visit the Land of Enchantment to experience the stunning beauty and rich history that will surround you at each turn.

ANCIENT CULTURES

The cultures that first developed New Mexico, thought primitive by many, were in fact quite sophisticated and accomplished for their time. The structures at Bonito Pueblo at Chaco Canyon are a prime example of this ingenuity.

Scientists have pinpointed the Clovis culture to the end of the last glacial period, over 11,000 years ago. It is believed that most of the indigenous people can call the hunter-gather Clovis people their ancestors. This information is derived from the 12,600-year-old skeleton of an infant boy, nicknamed "Anzick-1." It provided researchers with a wealth of DNA samples.

PUEBLOAN PEOPLE

The Tiwa people contributed much to the ancient cultures of the New World, developing complex communities and housing structures. Large apartment-like buildings, some as high as seven stories, were constructed by the Puebloan people as protection from marauding tribes who roamed the area. Windowless and doorless, the rooms were only entered using ladders. A single opening in a ceiling is the only access to the building below. Ladders were extracted for further protection during nighttime hours.

As with the case of Bonito Pueblo in northern New Mexico, the community was ruled by a single matriarchal family. Women were often the leaders of Puebloan societies but also did a vast majority of the everyday work needed to maintain the settlements.

TIGUEX WAR

King Philip II of Spain delegated Francisco Vásquez de Coronado to the New World in 1540 to find the legendary "Cities of Gold" to supply the much-depleted coffers of Spain with silver and gold. Coronado took his task to heart, setting out to accomplish the mission at any cost. One of the first Puebloan settlements the Coronado expedition encountered was Hawikuh Pueblo, close to today's Zuni Pueblo. The Spanish were quick to deplete the pueblo's food supply. Once the damage was done, the large group moved on to Tiguex (tee-wish), a largely peaceful community near present-day Bernalillo and ancestors to the Tewa people, who were also renowned for their finely woven cotton cloth and farming skills.

Coronado's army of nearly two thousand people forced its way into the settlement with a need for food, clothing and shelter. Not in the mood to barter with the people, Coronado's men looted anything they needed or wanted. The numerous herds of livestock diminished the dried cornstalks the Tiguex had stored for winter fuel and were let loose in the fields for grazing.

It was the assault on the wives of Tiguex men by a Spanish soldier that pushed the beleaguered tribe to the breaking point. In retaliation, the horses and mules of the Spaniards were killed, and a three-month battle between the Tiguex people and the Spanish interlopers ensued. Unfortunately for the natives, Coronado declared "a war of fire and blood," now known as the Tiguex War. Spain's tactics and weapons were too much for the Tiguex; most of the male population was killed, and the women and children were enslaved.

True to his word, Coronado also dispatched a large force of his men to attack a neighboring Tiwa village known as Arenal, where they proceeded to kill all of the village warriors, thirty of whom met the horrible fate of being burned alive at the stake. Due to these actions, the Tiwa abandoned their settlement on the Rio Grande and retreated to a nearby mesa to escape the violence. Over the course of three long winter months, the Tiguex people were starved out on the mesa, forcing them to concede and retreat down the mountain. Coronado and his men immediately took advantage of this maneuver by killing all the remaining men and most of the women, enslaving a small group of women until the Spaniards left the area in 1541. The Tiguex never recovered from this atrocity, the first of many to come.

ENTRADA OF 1598

Fifty-eight years later, in 1598, the Spanish explorers returned, under the leadership of Don Juan de Oñate y Salazar. The exact number of followers varies depending on the source, but it is generally stated that 126 soldiers, along with 8 to 10 priests, as well as hundreds of women, children and servants/slaves, made their way up the Rio Grande from Mexico to San Gabriel de Yunque-Ouinge in northern Nuevo Mexico to set their claim for Spain. The party included 83 wagons and 7,000 head of cattle and livestock. San Gabriel was the first Spanish capital of the provincial territory and was located west of present-day Ohkay Owingeh Pueblo (San Juan) at the confluence of the Rio Chama and Rio Grande. The original site was declared a National Historic Landmark in 1964. Unfortunately, it was plowed under in 1984, with only a historical marker remaining.

Since the Spanish Crown was still not convinced that the fabled "Cities of Gold" did not exist, it dispatched the Oñate expedition to finally locate and secure the great riches waiting to be plucked from the new land. After long wars with the British, Spain's coffers were greatly depleted. To pay the bills, the treasuries were in desperate need of replenishment. The New World, claimed for the Spanish Crown by the early explorers, was then the only salvation for the kingdom.

Oñate's contract with the Spanish Crown contained expedition priorities: "Your main purpose shall be the service of our Lord, the spreading of His Holy Catholic faith, and the reduction and pacification of the Natives of said provinces. You shall bend all your energies to this object, without any other human interest interfering with this aim."

Spain's colonial legislation called for the integration of the native population into the Spanish Empire. The papacy gave the Spanish Crown "title over the Indies, with the conditional obligation of carrying on the conversion of the aboriginal population." This mandate also included the right to collect tribute from the Puebloan people.

There were three objectives of the Spanish Crown in the conversion of the native people: "They desired to convert him, to civilize him, and to exploit him." These objectives were included in the "New Laws and Ordinances for the Government of the Indies," written in 1543. It set out to make the native people citizens of the Spanish Crown; however, they were never considered to be full citizens of the empire, only wards of the king. The natives were treated as children, patronized and considered too uncivilized to be true citizens. The Franciscan friars started with a noble goal; they were on a mission to save the souls of those they deemed "heathens" in the New World. Unfortunately, they became motivated by power and greed, leading to cruelty in many cases. Tactics used left a sour taste in the mouths and hearts of the Pueblo people for the invading strangers and their newly introduced religion.

The Entrada of 1598 forged the El Camino Real de Tierra Adentro (the Royal Road of the Interior Land), which would be used until the introduction of the railroad. Some of the present-day Interstate system in New Mexico follows this famous route. The El Camino Real stretched from deep within Mexico, starting at Mexico City, and reached the Tewa village, founded in the year 12 CE, of Ohkay Owingeh, which was commonly known as San Juan Pueblo and founded near the Rio Grande.

Original structures of the native pueblos were customized by the Spanish to a more familiar way of life for the conquering explorers, setting into motion great resentments and hatred from the Puebloan people. These feelings would soon reach a boiling point, and life would never be the same for native or intruder.

THE SPANISH MISSION AND CHURCHES

Missions were created to precipitate the conversion of the native people to the Catholic religion. It was the goal of the Spanish Crown, through its priests, to have a 100 percent conversion rate. This lofty goal was not reached, due to the fact that the tactics used to reach the goal included brutality, oppression of native rituals and enslavement. Differences between the cultures were immense, and the ancient traditions of the inhabitants of the pueblos were restricted. At times, if they were practiced, the participants could be punished with death. Baptism of all members of the native tribes was the goal of the Spanish Crown. The Pueblo people referred to the Spanish as "wet heads" after witnessing the baptismal ritual.

Under the direction of the Franciscan friars, who made the journey into the new land with the Spanish explorers, mission churches were constructed using native labor. These structures are 120 years older than the mission churches in Texas and 170 years older than the missions in California. Each pueblo in which a mission church was constructed was stripped of its native name and given a name of a saint to begin the conversion process. In recent years, several of the northern pueblos have reverted to their original names and traditions.

Most of the mission churches constructed throughout the New World were of similar design. Fashioned from adobe brick (a mud and straw mixture), the interior ceiling was covered in small wood branches (*latillas*) and large pine log beams. Generally, the floors were dirt, and several graves were traditionally underneath the feet of the parishioners sitting in the hard, straight back wooden pews. Kneelers, also made of wood, were added much later in the process. Before then, prayers were given while kneeling on the dirt floors. A large, painted wood altar screen, or reredos, adorned the wall behind the plain altar as well as the side walls. These were depicted with hand-painted scenes and portraits of the patron saint of the church (called *retablos*) in most cases.

PUEBLO REVOLT OF 1680

Oppression and cruelty experienced by the Tiwa people at the hands of the Spanish explorers were immense and pushed them to a breaking point. Their lands were invaded by a people who did not have the same religious or environmental views, and this led to many cultural conflicts.

In 1675, after religious rituals and the *kachinas* (Puebloan gods) were outlawed by the Franciscan friars, unrest began to emerge. Prayer sticks, figurines and masks of the Pueblo people were being destroyed and burned by the clergy, literally adding fuel to the already growing fire. A drought resulted in famine, which spread throughout New Mexico, sending tensions even higher. The inhabitants of this barren land were forced to eat cowhides and even leather straps from carts and grass for nourishment.

The tipping point came when Governor Juan Francisco Treviño declared that the medicine men of the pueblos were practicing sorcery and ordered them to be rounded up to face charges. Forty-seven men were arrested, with four sentenced to death immediately. Three of the medicine men were hanged, but the fourth committed suicide before his sentence was enacted. Forty-three medicine men were then publically flogged and sentenced to prison. As the news spread to the pueblos, their leaders went to Santa Fe and forced Governor Treviño to release the prisoners. He did so, as the majority of his soldiers were away fighting Apache raiders and the natives were troublesome.

From this group of prisoners, a religious leader from San Juan Pueblo—known today as Ohkay Owingeh—emerged who devised an ingenious plan to overthrow the Spanish rulers This came to be known as the Pueblo Revolt of 1680. Popé—or Po'pay, as he is commonly known (which means "ripe squash" in Tewa)—could not bear to see the abuse his people were having to endure at the hands of the Spanish. A small piece of deerskin rope adorned with knots played a huge role in the overthrow of the Spanish Crown in the New World.

From his home at Taos Pueblo, Popé, along with other Pueblo leaders, planned the revolt for five years. Popé dispatched runners carrying knotted ropes to all the pueblos. It was planned that the leaders would untie one knot each morning. When the last one was undone, it was time to rise up against the Spaniards. On August 9, Southern Tiwa Pueblos warned the Spanish of the impending revolt. In addition, two runners from Tesuque Pueblo were captured and tortured, revealing the significance of the knotted rope. These events only moved the revolt up two days.

As the siege began, the Spaniards took shelter in Santa Fe, only to have their water supply cut off, which created a desperate situation for the Europeans. Those taking refuge in Santa Fe were permitted to leave soon after the attack, but at the height of the revolt, over four hundred Spaniards were killed, including many women and children. Several thousand fled south to what is now the El Paso, Texas region. During the melee, twenty-one of the thirty-three priests were also killed. It was the intent of the native people to wipe every bit of the Spaniards' existence off their lands. Churches, records, books and religious affects were burned or destroyed. Many of the oldest mission churches were reduced to piles of burning rubble, leaving a blight on their land. This action went down in history as the first successful revolt in which an invading force was banished from a land for a great period.

A statue honoring the efforts of Po'pay was erected in the United States Capitol National Statuary Hall Collection in 1977. At seven feet tall, the statue, which is carved from pink marble from Tennessee by Jemez Pueblo sculptor Cliff Fragua, is the first to represent a person born on American soil.

RECONQUISTA OF 1692 AND THE REBELLION OF 1696

Once attitudes began to level out, life returned to normal, and the harsh memories of the events in 1680 began to slightly fade, although they were never forgotten. This allowed the Spaniards to begin a slow return to northern New Mexico in 1692, terming it a *Reconquista* (reconquer). The Puebloan people were leery of the Spanish settlers' return, but they were a peaceful people who initially did not raise much opposition to the resettlement. Historians argue that if the Puebloan people had fought back, the Spaniards may have left them alone for good and moved on.

Clear guidelines were set. The creators of the pueblos would not tolerate the treatment they had previously encountered. This led to a nonviolent existence between the two cultures. These guidelines were tossed by the wayside by the Spanish, however, after a few years, resulting in the poor conditions returning. This ill treatment was the direct cause of the Rebellion of 1696. Although not quite as bloody, the deaths of five missionaries and twenty-one settlers occurred in the six-month incursion, which had been poorly planned. Contributing factors to the rebellion besides the harsh treatment were the severe drought and famine conditions at the pueblos during this time.

MIXING OF CULTURES

It appears the indigenous people became resigned to the religious ways of the Spanish Crown, converting to the Catholic religion presented to them. Many are extremely devoted to this day. Tribal traditions are still strong and blend well with the adopted culture as many pueblos have reverted to their original language and names. Although sometimes repressed, the Puebloan people have always been able to preserve their culture for future generations to learn and enjoy.

MANIFEST DESTINY

As the United States took interest in the land to the west via the doctrine of Manifest Destiny, the lands of indigenous people became endangered once again. To advance the physical size and wealth of the United States, the doctrine of Manifest Destiny was drafted, stating basically that the American people were destined to confiscate lands in order to spread democracy and capitalism. It did not matter if these lands were already occupied and owned by other people and cultures. This document was instrumental in the destruction of the landholdings of Native Americans as well as early Mexican and Spanish settlers by allowing the United States to expand from the eastern to the western shores.

PUEBLO CULTURE TODAY

When you visit the pueblos, make the visitor center or tribal office your first point of contact to avoid any violations. (Both offices are closed on feast days; every pueblo has a different feast day, and you will find them listed in this book.) Celebrations and dances are held on most holidays recognized by the United States as well, such as New Year's Day, Easter, Memorial Day, Thanksgiving Day, Christmas Eve and Christmas Day. Although the pueblos are tourist destinations, they are also private homes. Each pueblo has its own governing body who set the rules and regulations for that site, but they are generally the same with a few exceptions. The Pueblo people are generous and welcoming, but please be mindful of these general rules and any others of the individual pueblos:

1. Do not take photographs of people and houses, unless invited.
2. Do not enter or take photographs of restricted areas.
3. Cameras and recording devices are forbidden in several locations, and permits are required at many pueblos. If you are caught violating the "no photo, no recording, no sketching" rule or doing these activities without a permit, you can find yourself having your camera, cellphone or art supplies confiscated without apology, never to be seen again.
4. During feast days, if you are invited to eat, accept the invitation, since it is an honor, but do not stand and talk for long periods of time. Residents will have many more mouths to feed.
5. Please do not stand in front of the Elders during feast day dances. Be as courteous as possible; you are a visitor at their home.
6. Obey all traffic, parking and speed limit signs.
7. Kivas and graveyards are not to be entered by non-Pueblo people.
8. Please keep children under control and ensure that they remain respectful.
9. Do not pick up, remove or disturb any artifact or object, such as broken pottery, plants, rocks or animals.
10. Do not bring alcohol, weapons, drugs or pets into Pueblo communities.
11. Do not climb walls or other structures, as they may be hundreds of years old and easily damaged.
12. Stay in the immediate village area; do not wander.

Please be respectful of the Pueblos as if you are walking through your own neighborhoods. Respect is always key.

New Mexico pueblos are known for their talented artists. Fine silver and turquoise jewelry, painted and sculpted pottery, weavings, rugs and hand-carved stone fetishes are but some of the products available for purchase from most of the pueblos that have gift shops or in Gallup, Santa Fe or Albuquerque. Each pueblo has a distinctive style, and it is easy to distinguish each from just a glance and with a small amount of study.

Several Pueblo artists have become famous for their artwork, such as Maria Martinez of San Ildefonso, the most famous Pueblo potter. Maria and her husband, Julian, invented the striking black-on-black work, which is highly sought after and increasing in value daily. Maria's pottery has sold at recent auctions for $225,000 and more and has had the honor of being part of the White House art collection. As you visit the magnificent examples of Puebloan life available to you in the Land of Enchantment, it will be hard not to be amazed at the ingenuity, history, architecture and culture displayed before you, appearing much as it did in ancient times. Take time to absorb the healing vibes of the earth and sky, but be warned, New Mexico will always be with you no matter where you roam.

PART I

PUEBLO MISSIONS

Chapter 1

ISLETA

"Flint Kick-Stick Place"
Traditional name: Tue-I
Pronunciation: IS-let-ah
Feast day: August 28

Fifteen miles south of Albuquerque, the largest city in New Mexico, sits the quiet village of Isleta. Set against the beautiful Manzano Mountains, the ancient city was named Isleta ("Little Island") by the Spanish explorers who came to the region. The native people called their village Shiewhibak ("Shee-whib-bac"), which translates, "a knife laid on the ground to play whib." Whib is a popular native footrace.

Lady in Blue

One of the most interesting legends surrounding Isleta Pueblo is that of the Lady in Blue, or the Blue Nun. Stories circulated throughout the region of a female missionary dressed in blue who taught the Pueblo people the ways of the Catholic Church before some of the Spanish expeditions had reached the isolated settlements.

Franciscan friars who arrived in the area with Spanish explorers were astonished to learn that the Jumano Indians who resided near the site of

Isleta Pueblo sits fifteen miles from New Mexico's largest city, Albuquerque, and is also home to a four-star golf course, casino and resort.

the present-day Isleta Pueblo, near the Salinas Missions, already had a good grip on the fundamentals of the Catholic religion. When questioned as to the reason, they all mentioned the lady in blue garments who would appear to them to teach the ways of the faith in their own language. The mysterious lady would distribute rosaries to the tribe and encouraged them to seek the counsel of the nearest Puebloan Franciscan friars. When these priests were told of the over five hundred spiritual visits by the "Lady in Blue," an investigation was begun.

At first, the friars were convinced the visitor was the Virgin Mary, but they came to realize soon enough she was not, although her name was María. Sister María Jesús de Ágreda was a member of the Poor Clare sisters in north-central Spain but was raised in a noble family. Her mother, Catherine, had received what she termed a vision to renounce their noble status and convert their castle into a Poor Clare convent, where she and her two daughters were to reside. Catherine's husband was to enter a monastery with their sons. Catherine saw to it this vision was realized. This convent was called the Franciscan Convent of the Immaculate Conception at Ágreda.

The Blue Nun said she visited the people of Isleta with the help of angels.

It was in this convent that María worked, prayed and did work for the poor. It was also where she began to reach high levels of piety and mysticism through her devotion. María experienced mockery from other members of the convent, sending the young nun into a state of despair and physical deterioration. After an ecclesiastical examination was done of María, it was determined that she had reached true sanctity. Hearing this, the mother superior was shamed by the way María was treated. So much so, they began to hold her in such high esteem, which was embarrassing to the nun.

María began to have trance-like episodes in 1620 during which she claimed to visit the Jumanos Indians in the New World to teach them about the Catholic religion in what the church would later call "bi-location." It was said that María would visit the native tribe of New Mexico sometimes two and three times daily. It had become her goal to save the souls of the tribal members. She said that she would give her life to save just one Indian soul.

Reports of María's visits spread throughout Spain and to the Holy Office of the Spanish Inquisition, which sent out inquiries to the New World to substantiate the nun's claims. Although the priests had not heard of María or of her visits, when they asked the tribal members, much to their astonishment, they were told of a lady in blue visiting them over the years and teaching them the ways of the Catholic Church. After several investigations both in New Mexico and Spain, María's claims were found to be true.

María authored *The Mystical City of God,* a 2,676-page (eight books, six volumes) extremely detailed account of her mystical voyages throughout the years in which she said she was "transported by the aid of angels." This book drew the unwanted attention of the Inquisition and put the nun in an unwelcomed limelight. Luckily, María was not treated poorly by the Inquisition Council, which was known for its brutality, most likely because of her relationship with and intercession by King Philip IV on her behalf, approving her book after fourteen years of study. The book was banned from circulation by the Vatican, but this restriction was lifted in 1747.

Visitations by María to the pueblos were reported by inhabitants throughout the Southwest into the twentieth century, although María had succumbed to death in 1665. Reports state that in the three centuries since Sister María Jesús de Ágreda's death, her body has shown no signs of decay. Due to María's great works and abilities, sainthood for the "Blue Nun" has been mentioned on two occasions, but with no success. Of course, there are skeptics of this story, but it has been well documented in tribal and church lore.

MISSION SAN AGUSTIN DE ISLETA

St. Augustine Church in Isleta Pueblo has the honor of being one of two of the oldest mission churches in New Mexico, as well as America's oldest active parish. Construction of the mission church by the people of Isleta began in 1613, after the Spanish Entrada of 1598, with Don Juan de Oñate in the lead. It was completed in 1617. At that time, the mission was dedicated to San Antonio de Padua, which serviced upward of seven thousand pueblo members, who were all reported to have been baptized by two Franciscan friars assigned to the pueblo.

This version of the mission church was burned (except for the nave), as was all other evidence of Spanish existence in New Mexico during the Pueblo Revolt of 1680. It was rebuilt in 1716 on the original foundation.

As with all real estate, location is key, as it certainly was in Isleta's case. It was situated across the river from the El Camino Real (the Royal Highway), which was the major trade route from Mexico connecting with the rest of the pueblos and settlements in the region. Today, Isleta Pueblo is still in a good location, only fifteen miles from Albuquerque, the largest city in New Mexico.

Left: Bells of most mission churches have cracks, a result of being struck in extreme weather conditions. *Right*: Hand-carved wood doors crafted by parish members offer beauty and protection.

The interior of the centrally located mission church was plain and simply built, consisting of wood latillas on the ceiling above the altar, a collection of hand-carved wood crucifixes, *santos* and *retablos*. As with most early mission interiors, it featured whitewashed plaster walls. By 1885, wood floors had been added, along with an iron stove for heat and a wood confessional booth.

Today, parishioners describe St. Augustine as one of the most spiritual churches in New Mexico. They are pleased to be able to celebrate using both traditional and Catholic ways.

Pueblo Revolt

The oppression of the Spanish rule took a toll on the native population, who were often used as slaves to build churches and work in the fields and forced give the majority of their stockpiles for winter storage to the Spanish invaders. Isleta was one of the few pueblos that did not participate in the revolt but were allied with the Spanish and provided shelter to the Spanish settlers and Pueblo people fleeing for their lives.

This created animosity with the rest of the pueblos, and Isleta Pueblo was shunned for a time after the revolt. Many of the residents of Isleta followed the Spanish to El Paso, establishing Ysleta del Sur Pueblo there. Others headed to Arizona to join the Hopi settlements, where many took Hopi spouses, creating a new culture when they returned to New Mexico. This situation was not met with great enthusiasm from the Isleta Pueblo, but they were tolerant.

Isleta Pueblo owns and operates the Isleta Resort and Casino, which provides gaming opportunities, concert venues, a bowling alley, room accommodations and dining for all who come through its doors. With a staff of sixty-five people, the resort generates $65 million in sales each year and is the main support for the Isleta Pueblo.

CHAPTER 2

ZIA

"Sun Symbol"
Traditional name: Tsi-ya
Pronunciation: ZEE-ah
Feast day: August 15

Within a stone's throw of Bernalillo, a suburb of Albuquerque, Zia Pueblo is the creator of New Mexico's state symbol, the Zia. The number four is sacred for the Zia Pueblo, which is represented in multiple ways in the symbol's rays: the four seasons of life (childhood, youth, middle years and old age); the four seasons (spring, summer, fall and winter); times of the day (sunrise, noon, evening and night); and the four directions (north, east, south and west). The Zia people believe in "the giver of all good," who gave them the gifts represented in the groups of four.

The Zia symbol was adopted by the State of New Mexico as its official symbol, to be emblazoned on the state flag, in 1925. The official salute to the New Mexico flag is as follows, "I salute the flag of the state of New Mexico, the Zia symbol of perfect friendship among united cultures." In order to honor New Mexico's statehood, the U.S. government minted the state's quarter, which proudly displayed the Zia symbol in 2008 as the forty-seventh coin, to coincide with New Mexico being the forty-seventh state admitted to the Union. Unfortunately, due to the ubiquity within regional representation, the Zia tribe is prohibited from obtaining a legal trademark under federal law for the highly recognizable symbol. The Zia was recently

Exterior of Nuestra Señora de Asunción Church at Zia Pueblo features painted images of a horse. *Library of Congress.*

removed from the flag of Madison, Wisconsin, where it had been from 1962 to 2018. Madison removed the symbol after concerns of tribal, Puebloan and New Mexican cultural appropriation were raised.

Zia Pueblo sits in the Sierra Nacimiento Mountains along the Jemez River, thirty-five miles northwest of Albuquerque and sixteen miles northwest of Bernalillo on New Mexico Highway 44. It is listed in the National Register of Historic Places. The pueblo itself sits proudly on top of a mesa, but if you visit, please follow all rules posted at the gate. Note that photography is not allowed. Should you be caught taking photos or videos or sketching images, all your equipment will be confiscated, including cellphones. Zia Pueblo is sacred to the Zia people, and although it is open to visitors during the daylight hours, it is a private pueblo that holds to strict traditions.

First noticed by Spanish explorer Antonio de Espejo in 1583, Zia was recorded as the largest pueblo. It was called Tsiya by the native population but named Punames by the Spaniards. The name was later changed also by the Spanish to Zia. It was described as having eight large plazas surrounded by over one thousand two- and three-story houses that held a population from five thousand to possibly twenty thousand. This population would be diminished in the coming years by battles, drought, famine and rebellion.

Above: The Zia sun, adopted as New Mexico's state symbol, was originally found on Zia Pueblo pottery.

Left: A Buffalo Dancer from Zia Pueblo. *Library of Congress*.

These numbers would never be completely replenished until the twentieth century. Reduced to two plazas and a population of approximately three hundred residents, Zia Pueblo is a proud, yet private, community.

As with the other pueblos, Zia residents believed in guiding spirits, called *kachinas*, who are believed to be spirits of their ancestors that live among the people. Legend states the kachinas became offended when the people began to ignore them, so they returned to the sky to live, only to return in the form of clouds or rain. There are over three hundred kachinas in the worship system of the Pueblos, utilized in dances by religious men.

As the site of a bloody skirmish between the conquistadors and the people of Zia, the pueblo was attacked by Governor Domingo Jironza Pétriz de Cruzate in 1689. Six hundred tribal members lost their lives, and seventy were taken captive by the Spanish, to be held in El Paso for the next ten years. It was after this incident that Zia Pueblo moved several miles northward. When Diego de Vargas returned in 1692, the Zia people offered no resistance when he requested they return to their original residence.

NUESTRA SEÑORA DE ASUNCIÓN CHURCH

Construction on an early version of the Nuestra Señora de Asunción (Our Lady of the Assumption) Church began in 1598, when the Spanish expedition of Don Juan de Oñate arrived in northern New Mexico to begin the conversion of native inhabitants to the Catholic faith by Fray Alonso de Lugo, who was placed in charge of the Zia Pueblo. It is thought the *convento* was built by tribal members under the instruction of Fray Cristobal de Quiros in 1610, but the first church was completed in 1613, also build by pueblo residents and given the name Saint Pedro y Saint Pablo by Oñate.

Facing eastward on the mesa, Nuestra Señora de Asunción Church has seen times of disrepair, turmoil and dysfunction. Damage incurred to the church during the Pueblo Revolt of 1680 caused the structure to be rebuilt starting in 1692 by Fray Juan Alpuente, who was assigned to Zia. Construction was finished in 1704 by the returning Franciscan friars.

Heavy logs were cut and hauled down from the surrounding mountains to be used for roofing materials for the new church. Thousands of adobe bricks were then crafted by residents to enlarge the church into the structure we see today. Unfortunately, the scourge of smallpox spread through the

Kivas are sacred meeting places used for centuries. *Library of Congress.*

pueblo, dramatically reducing the population by 1892, to the point where only 120 residents remained.

Preservation became an issue in the 1920s, when the Committee for the Preservation and Restoration of the New Mexican Mission Churches came into existence. In 1923, the addition of electric lighting, a concrete slab for a new roof and fresh stucco allowed pueblo members to utilize the church. By the 1970s, Zia Pueblo added electricity and gas heating panels to the interior for the comfort of parishioners. Although the convento is no longer in existence, the church with its cemetery remains and was able to escape the modernization in the 1920s that was so popular. Nuestra Señora de Asunción Church was made a priority by the Restoration Committee in 1923.

The rotting vigas were replaced with fresh roofing paper and copper-lined canals, moving the water away from the ceiling and building, which tended to leak. Standing on the highest point of the basalt mesa, shining white, Nuestra Señora de la Asunción Church can be seen from Highway 550, thirty miles north of Albuquerque, as the most prominent structure in the pueblo. Today's church has a new layer of smooth, light-colored stucco applied with colorful painted images of horses on the front façade balcony. Preservation on this National Register of Historic Places church is evident in how well the church appears—the years of neglect have been pressed out.

Horses were an extremely important aspect of Pueblo life after they were introduced to the native people by the Spanish in 1598. Paintings of horses adorn the front façade of the mission church, representing the mixture of Spanish and native cultures.

Zia Pueblo has also been used as a setting for several films, including *Dead & Alive*, *Desperado II*, *Earth 2* and *New Eden*. The pueblo is also known for its intricate pottery designs, especially during the Trios period. After 1900, the designs included floral images and Zia birds, but today the patterns are more geometric, with a heavy influence of the Zia sun symbol.

Directions: Thirty-five miles northwest of Albuquerque and sixteen miles northwest of Bernalillo off Highway 550 on Highway 44.

Chapter 3

NAMBÉ

"People of the Round Earth"
Traditional name: Nambé Owingeh (Nambe-O-ween-Ge)
Pronunciation: nahm-BAY
Feast day: October 4

Twenty miles north of the oldest capital city in the United States (Santa Fe), Nambé Pueblo is now famous for its beautiful pottery, textiles and waterfalls and was settled in the early fourteenth century. Nestled in the foothills of the Sangre de Cristo Mountains, the twenty thousand acres of land covered with cottonwoods, juniper and scrub oak are surrounded by red sandstone outcroppings. The Rio Nambé cuts a path through the pueblo as it rushes from the headwaters five miles to the east of the reservation border and empties into the Rio Grande, providing much-needed water for the village.

One of the eight northern pueblos, Nambé played a role in planning the Pueblo Revolt of 1680. The mistreatment of the indigenous people was widespread throughout the state, leading to unrest and resentment among the northern tribes.

Nambé Pueblo is a self-governing tribe recognized by the federal government, organized under the Indian Reorganization Act of June 18, 1934, and remains to be organized in accordance with Pueblo tradition. Nambé Pueblo is separate from the community of Nambé, which is surrounded by Hispanic villages and is listed in the U.S. National Register of Historic Places and the New Mexico State Register of Cultural Properties. It is also a United States Historic District.

SAGRADA CORAZÓN DE JESÚS

This striking church has a long history of highs and lows. Built in 1618, it was destroyed in the Pueblo Revolt of 1680. Once the Spaniards returned in 1696, the community built a second church, which turned out to be too small for the congregation. A third, larger church was completed in 1790 and was christened Sagrada Corazón de Jesús (Sacred Heart of Jesus). It burned in the early 1900s and was rebuilt in 1910. This church was also ill-fated, as it burned down during Holy Week in 1945. It was quickly rebuilt in the present adobe style with twin buttresses and bell towers.

Today, the church looks much like it did when it was rebuilt. Heavy pine log beams and corbels line the length of the ceiling, used as support for multiple weighty iron chandeliers that provide light for the sanctuary. Stations of the Cross line the whitewashed interior of the church. A marble altar is at the north end of the church and features a large statue of the Sacred Heart of Jesus. This statue is flanked by smaller statues of the Virgin Mary on the right and St. Joseph on the left, with angels bowing at His feet. Pine plank floors and pews add warmth to the structure for the parishioners. Stained-glass windows provide spectacular light shows in the interior at both sunrise and sunset.

A touching tribute, as one grave in the Nambé cemetery has the exact replica of the church.

Belfries of the Sacred Heart of Jesus Christ Church in Nambé.

The Sacred Heart Catholic Church at Nambé is on the High Road to Taos and backs up to Highway 508. During Holy Week, thousands of pilgrims pass by the church, mostly on foot, on their way to El Santuario de Chimayó in Chimayó, nearly eight miles away. Breathtaking views from the parking lot surround this quaint church. Coyote fencing, chamisa and wildflowers line the narrow scenic highway, creating a feast for the eye.

Take note of the small cemetery on the right-hand side of the road as you exit Highway 508, which is filled with colorful flowers, beads and tinsel and gives the cemetery an almost festive feel as the living celebrate the lives of their loved ones who have passed on. One grave marker stands out, as it is an exact replica of Sacred Heart of Jesus Church.

Home to one of the "most spectacular natural waterfalls in the southwest," according to the pueblo website, Nambé Falls is part of a recreation area that provides hiking, camping and fishing for its visitors. Fees are charged for use of facilities; tickets are available at the visitor center.

Photography permits are required and can be obtained from the tribal center, but there is no admission fee to view the pueblo.

Chapter 4

PECOS

Traditional name: Cicuyé or Tziquite

Just off Interstate 25, twenty-six miles from Santa Fe, lies the small but important historic town of Pecos, New Mexico. "Just six miles off the beaten path" is the motto used by the town as it lures travelers off the interstate. Sheltered in a scenic valley in the breathtaking Sangre de Cristo Mountains with high-desert piñons, juniper and ponderosa pine, the tiny village of Pecos (or Cicuyé, as the Pueblo people called it) has had a long and historic past in New Mexico. Long used as a cultural and supply route by indigenous people as well as by Spanish and Angelo explorers, the village's ten thousand years of rich history is preserved at the Pecos National Historical Park, which houses the Pecos Pueblo and Mission. It was once known as Levy, the Spanish equivalent for the Keresan word for "place where there is water."

Mission Nuestra Señora de Los Ángeles de Porciúncula

Once you turn off the busy interstate, you will be embraced with a sense of peace. Stunning vistas along the Old Santa Fe Trail and Historic Route 66 tempt you to slow down and enjoy. Pecos, New Mexico, has several

High above the visitor center at Pecos National Historical Site is the remnant of one of the largest mission churches of its era.

Sacred to the Pueblo People, kivas are places for ritual and tradition.

attractions to offer on the way in or out of the Pecos National Historic Park. Part of the 1600s "Golden Age of Missions," Mission Nuestra Señora de Los Ángeles de Porciúncula (Mission of Our Lady of the Angels of Porciuncula) was built around 1619 as the first church erected by Fray Pedro Zambrano Ortiz.

The residents of Cicuyé (Pecos) Pueblo, the largest and richest in New Mexico at that time, would not allow a Spanish church to be built near their sacred buildings, so the mission was erected 440 yards northeast of the main quadrangle of the pueblo configuration. By 1621, Fray Andres Juarez, a healer and builder, saw the need for a more permanent structure, which led to the construction of another church outside the pueblo walls. This structure was an imposing sight, with six towers, including dual bell towers in the front, huge pine beams that had been hauled in from the surrounding mountains and multiple buttresses along the length of the church building.

Mission Nuestra Señora de Los Angeles de Porcuincula is a beautiful ruin from the "Golden Age of Missions."

Often described as a megachurch because of the five thousand square feet it encompassed and the imposing twenty-foot walls that rose from the red soil, Pecos Pueblo was seen by its neighbors as a powerful, dominant fortress.

Even though this building ushered in the mission period and Pecos was considered a royal colony, the strife between the pueblo inhabitants and the Spanish soon began. The natives were forced to work for the Spanish, to pay tribute (which included much of their food stock) and to pledge loyalty to a god they did not know or want. Those who were loyal to the Spanish were said to have warned the priests of the upcoming revolt, but most followed the tribal elders in the revolt and killed the priests. Unfortunately, the large church was then burned to the ground and destroyed during the Pueblo Revolt of 1680.

Once the Spanish settlers began to trickle back into the Pecos wilderness during the Reconquista of 1692, they began to reinsert their religious beliefs into the indigenous culture. Mindsets had changed by this time. The Pecos Pueblo accepted Diego de Vargas on his arrival and supplied him with 140 warriors to help with the Reconquista of Santa Fe.

Using the stone foundation and existing walls of the destroyed church, a small church was built in 1717, the third erected on this spot. At this point, the Franciscan friars had started to see the error of some of their ways and discontinued the practice of demanding *encomiendas* (paying tribute) but, regrettably, continued with indentured servitude, to at a lesser degree. These changes led to a more peaceful coexistence between the cultures.

Ruins of the smaller church, three thousand square feet in size, which replaced the burned megachurch, is what we see today at the Pecos National Historical Park. The remaining architecture is stunning. Archaeologists have found intricate tile of the finest quality during their excavations.

End of an Era

By 1838, the Pecos Pueblo had been abandoned, mainly as a result of disease, drought, migration and raids by the Comanche tribe. Hispanic ranches were utilizing much of the farmland, which made growing their crops increasingly difficult. The Pecos Pueblo lost its functionality when its use as a trade center faded. By the time the Santa Fe Trail (ruts of which can still be seen in parts of the park) came through the area in 1821, the pueblo was in ruins. A few remaining residents moved to the Jemez Pueblo in 1838, leaving the deserted church and pueblo to the elements.

Glorieta Pass, the site of one of the largest battles of the Civil War, dubbed the "Gettysburg of the West."

During the Civil War, the region played a huge part in what was called the "Gettysburg of the West." Nearby Glorieta Pass Battlefield was a hot spot for the battle of the West to prevent the Confederate army from taking over the gold fields of New Mexico and Colorado and the Union fort of Fort Union. Cannonballs can still be seen embedded in boulders at the roadside exhibit of the Battle of Glorieta Pass on the way to the Pecos monument.

Today, a well-manicured, 1.25-mile self-guided walking path winds its way through the remaining ruins of Pecos National Historical Park. Please know that there is a shorter path to the church ruins for those who may have a hard time walking that distance—just take a left at the *Y* as you leave the beautiful museum/gift shop. Pecos National Historical Park was declared a National Historic Landmark on October 9, 1960.

Chapter 5

PICURIS

"Mountain Warrior Place" or "Mountain Pass Place"
Traditional name: Pe'ewi, or P'iwweltha
Spanish name: Pikuria ("People Who Paint")
Pronunciation: peec-Kuhr-Rees
Feast day: August 10

Picuris Pueblo is burrowed deep in what the people like to call a hidden valley of the Sangre de Cristo Mountains (Blood of Christ). People migrated there around CE 1250 from the Pot Creek Cultural Site, a large pueblo of over four hundred rooms and with a population of nearly three thousand souls near Taos, New Mexico. It is believed through archaeological evidence and folklore that some of the inhabitants of Chaco Canyon (Anasazi) in northwestern New Mexico also migrated east to the Taos Valley about this time, so some speculate that this may be the reason the Picuris people moved on. Another factor may have been the devastating fire that destroyed the southern portion of the site in 1320. No written history from the Anasazi was left, and the Picuris people follow the ways of the Anasazi.

The pueblo was named Pikuria ("those who paint") by Spanish conquistador Don Juan de Oñate, who had heard the Jemez Pueblo residents use a Tewa name, Pekwiles, to describe the Picuris. But the meaning given by the Pueblo people for themselves is "mountain warrior place." During excavations of Picuris Pueblo, colorful murals were found painted on the walls of the kiva. Such murals had previously been found only at the Kuaua Pueblo (Coronado Historical Site) and Pottery Mound. These murals, depicting lightning bolts, birds, rainbows and terraced pyramids, were thought to have been painted over a span of five hundred years.

Picuris Pueblo comprised eleven areas and was broken down into ceremonial societies in which persons (men of the pueblo) were either born or chosen for. These societies were the Spring People, Fall People, Winter People, Summer People and the Picuris Clown Society. There was a Hunt Chief and a Scalp Man, the latter a big chief of warriors who was the curator of the scalp house, where scalps were stored.

The Scalp Man also presided over the Scalp Dance. Scalps were observed hanging from the rafters in the upper chamber of the scalp house as late as 1910. It is reported that under the Scalp Man, the returning warriors formed a temporary warrior society, much like the Taos Warrior Society. Women were not allowed in the societies but volunteered to serve the society of their choice. According to the Picuris men, the women "were put here to serve the society, so they were serving."

During excavations, cache pits of traditional pueblo articles were found. Eagle claws, kiva bells, flutes, whistles and figurines were inventoried as items that may have been stashed by the early Pueblo people away from the judgmental eyes of the Franciscan friars, who had outlawed their traditional use.

SAN LORENZO MISSION

The picturesque setting on the banks of the Rio Pueblo is home to the smallest of the nineteen pueblos of New Mexico, with a population of only 334, but it has a rich cultural heritage. One of the centerpieces of the historical buildings is the two-hundred-year-old San Lorenzo Mission, which was restored using the original materials and methods handed down for centuries. Hand-formed adobe brick, mud and straw help to fortify the exterior of the beautiful mission church. The interior features examples of beautiful craftsmanship in hand-hewn corbel and vigas.

Cruciform in design, San Lorenzo Mission Church features thick adobe walls covered in stucco, a wall belfry, a wood portal, a stepped wall surrounding the cemetery, a church and a convent. Pottery produced by Picuris Pueblo has an unusual sheen, almost like copper, a result of the mica in the clay. Bean pots are the most popular of the pueblo's creations. Carl Tsosie, a tribal member, said that, much like the clay, "our faith is drawn from the earth."

Built between the years 1621 and 1629, San Lorenzo was the product of Fray Francisco de Zamora's assignment to establish a permanent mission in Picuris. As with other mission churches in the area, San Lorenzo was destroyed during the Pueblo Revolt of 1680 and fell to disuse afterward. After a devastating attack by the Comanche, who sacked the mission in 1769, the church was moved closer to the pueblo. Construction continued in 1776, with the convento completed in 1780.

San Lorenzo Mission saw total neglect in the nineteenth century, when it was untouched by priests or residents. By the 1930s, a new pitched tin roof had been added to preserve the church, but the building was torn nearly completely down by 1960 in order for the pueblo to rebuild it, this time returning the original flat roof. Portions of the nave wall collapsed in 1986, requiring major restoration.

A large bison herd is being raised by Picuris Pueblo to maintain their strong spiritual connection with the animals. The Pueblo website states, "Picuris is helping to restore the bison as both a food source and traditional spiritual enhancement for its people." They are proud to announce that the herd's number is upward of fifty and still increasing. The public can view the herd as it roams the beautiful valley.

The main industry of the Picuris Pueblo is the production of charcoal, which residents claim burns hotter and cleaner than briquettes. As a proactive effort to prevent devastating forest fires, the pueblo is thinning the surrounding forest to help maintain a healthy environment. Most of the charcoal comes from juniper, piñon, ponderosa, encino oak and ponderosa ocate. While harvesting the wood, invasive plants and hazardous growth are cut out to help restore the forest and maintain a defense against wildfires.

To see and photograph San Lorenzo Mission Church, one must obtain a permit for a small fee from the Picuris Smoke Shop at 1378 NM 75 in Peñasco, New Mexico. These permits help to support the small pueblo as well as aid with restoration attempts. This picturesque pueblo is along the banks of the Rio Pueblo and surrounded by mountain meadows teeming with wildflowers, grasses and multiple varieties of trees. Located sixty miles north of Santa Fe and twenty-four miles southeast of Taos, Picuris Pueblo is a feature on the High Road to Taos.

Chapter 6

JEMEZ

"This Is the Place"
Traditional name: Walatowa (a Towa word)
Pronunciation (traditionally): He-mish or Hay-mess
Feast day: August 2

Pine-tree-covered red sandstone mesas surround the ruins of the Jemez Pueblo, situated near the Jemez River. In the fall, the golden leaves of the numerous cottonwoods on the banks of the river glisten in the breeze, adding a subtle sparkle to the already colorful landscape. Words such as *stunning*, *serene* and *spectacular* are used to describe Jemez Springs on the village's website, and they are 100 percent accurate.

The history of the Jemez Pueblo is long and ranges from the ancient culture of the Puebloan people to the Spanish conquistadors to the modern, wonderfully relaxing hot springs. One fact that Jemez Springs is famous for may be a surprise to many: Bigfoot sightings. Apparently, Bigfoot knows a good place to relax and has become the unofficial mascot of Jemez Springs. T-shirt vendors attest to the validity of the sightings.

As you travel the narrow two-lane Highway 4 through the quaint village, you will be taken by the beauty of ancient settlements, striated hillsides and history that surrounds you. Jemez Springs has two excellent eateries, a brewery and several art galleries for your enjoyment, but the main attractions of the tiny town are the hot springs. Fed by the volcanic activity in the region, the springs provide a source of income for the town and are a healthful

Jemez Pueblo is surrounded by red rock walls, out of which the pueblo was built.

destination. In fact, the Jemez Springs municipal buildings use geothermal heat. A pool of warm water boasting seventeen different minerals offers a spot to unwind, relax and unplug from the world around you.

Jemez Springs is a tight-knit community. Up to 70 percent of the population still lived on the Jemez Reservation in the 1970s. It is mostly an agricultural society, where the residents still raise wheat, corn and chili peppers to survive. Some people have moved on to more lucrative jobs in the surrounding cities of Albuquerque and Santa Fe. The pueblo's residents are also known for their love of running. Used as a pastime and for ritual activity, running has become a popular sport for the community. In the 1950s, Indian tribes held track meets. Participants from Jemez Pueblo won the competition seven years out of ten. Steve Gachupin of Jemez set a record in 1968 when he won the Pikes Peak Marathon, reaching the top in two hours, fourteen minutes and fifty-six seconds. Gachupin would go on to win the marathon six times in his career.

Originating from a place called "Hua-na-tota," the Jemez people migrated to the San Diego Canyon region from the Four Corners area sometime in the thirteenth century. Jemez Pueblo is proud to say it grew to be one of the largest and most powerful Puebloan cultures in the high mountains of northern New Mexico. The stone structures, which were at times four stories high and contained over three thousand rooms, stretched for miles, making the area one of the largest archaeological sites in the United States. It is said that the location of the pueblo within the walls of the surrounding high mesas allowed for strategic defense against marauding tribes, resulting in a near-military society, so much so that Jemez Pueblo leaders were consulted in matters of war by the leaders of surrounding pueblos.

San Jose de los Jemez Church

The mission, established by the Spanish in the seventeenth century in San Diego Canyon, proved to be short-lived. It was abandoned and moved to the current location in Jemez Pueblo. San Jose de los Jemez Church, originally called Giusewa, was thought to have been built in 1621 or 1622. The name *Giusewa* refers to the natural hot springs in the area. The springs provide income for modern residents. As Spaniards began to settle northward, Jemez Pueblo encountered its first European in 1541, when the Coronado expedition traveled through the lands. It would be another forty years

This kiva at Jemez Pueblo is accessed by a wooden ladder.

before contact would again be made by the conquistadors, in the form of the Rodriguez-Chamuscado expedition (it found Jemez Pueblo in 1581), the Espejo expedition in 1583 and, finally, the Oñate expedition in 1598.

Fray Alonzo de Lugo was positioned in Jemez, where he used the thirty-thousand-strong Jemez Pueblo to build the church at the pueblo. With the new explorers came disease and unrest, resulting in many revolts as the Franciscan friars attempted to "Christianize" the Pueblo people, denying and outlawing all articles used in their native rituals. These rules resulted in the deaths of both Puebloan people and priests.

The convento and church were built in the traditions of the Pueblo practices, in which the Jemez women were tasked with building a huge church out of cut yellow limestone covered with plaster. This church was unusual in respect of its size and octagonal bell tower.

Resistance to the ill treatment given by the Franciscan friars resulted in 1630 in the deaths of three of the five missionaries at Hawikuh and Awatovi. These actions caused the priests to withdraw from these missions, leaving them empty around 1639. The focus turned toward San Diego de Jemez. After the Pueblo Revolt of 1680, the mission and Giusewa Pueblo fell into ruins. Attention was not given to San Jose de los Jemez Church until a land survey in 1849, when the thirty-nine-foot parapet walls were recorded. After excavation, two hundred ground-floor rooms, three Pueblo kivas and two plazas were uncovered at the original Giusewa Pueblo.

Today, the beautiful yellow and red rocks of the ruins are in bright contrast to the dark-green piñons and juniper trees that surround the site. Paved trails weave through the mission and pueblo site, where you can experience the full impact of the enormity of the building created by the pueblo women.

Being fifty-five miles northwest of the city of Albuquerque and an hour and twenty minutes southwest of Santa Fe, Jemez Springs, which was once known as Giggling Springs, is a delightful day trip. You can visit the 89,000 acres of land that house an approximate population of 3,400 tribal members. You can visit the Abousleman House, which is the most popular bathhouse at the springs. It is rumored that this house was used by the Federal Bureau of Investigation as its headquarters at one time. As one of the remaining nineteen pueblos in the Land of Enchantment, the Jemez Pueblo is a federally recognized tribe and has been designated a National Historic Landmark.

Chapter 7

SANTA CLARA

"Singing Water Village," also known as "Village of Wild Roses"
Traditional name: Kha' Po Owingeh
Feast day: August 12

Santa Clara Pueblo is world famous for its exquisite pottery, primarily made by the women of the pueblo. Black and red polished pottery featuring incised and sgraffito designs to make the pots look like melons is the distinctive style of the well-known potters.

Ancient Puebloans lived where the present-day pueblo is as far back as 1200 BC. They were isolated from other people until 1541, when a fragment of the Coronado expedition encountered the residents of the Caypa Pueblo (known today as Ohkay Owingeh, or San Juan) in their search for gold and treasures. The pueblo was annexed into the Spanish Kingdom, when Don Juan de Oñate made his expedition north from Mexico to establish settlements for the Spanish Crown. It was then that Oñate founded his colonial capital while directing the Franciscan friars who traveled with him to build a chapel in 1617. Under the direction of Fray Alonso de Benavides, a mission was formed in 1628, but it would be abandoned before the Great Pueblo Revolt of 1680.

Located one mile east of the present-day city of Española, New Mexico, Santa Clara Pueblo includes the Puye Cliff Dwellings of Pajarito Plateau, which are ten miles from the pueblo. These dwellings are touted as a "famed historical and archaeological landmark" near the pueblo of Santa Clara. The Puye Cliff Dwellings were home to a population of fifteen hundred residents

Traditional glazed black pottery was used to carry water from the source to the pueblo. *Library of Congress.*

between the AD 900s and 1580 and can be toured. You will find a two-level cliff-and-cave dwelling over a mile long at the base of the high cliff face. The upper level is about 2,100 feet long and is accessed by stairs and paths cut into the rock surfaces. Structures on the top level of the cliffs resemble a pueblo configuration with a single, multistoried complex surrounding a common central plaza. The exact number of rooms in the pueblo are unknown, but 173 have been found and excavated on the southern end of the settlement.

Famed archaeologist Edgar Lee Hewett was the first to excavate this fascinating site in the summer of 1907. Hewett found with the eruption of the volcano in the Valles Caldera, layers of basalt and volcanic tuff rained down and formed the sheer cliffs where the Puye Cliff Dwellings are located. Ancient settlers were able to dig into the tuff with stone tools to make living quarters and storage areas in the rock.

An unusual fact about the Puye Cliff Dwellings is that it is the only Native American reservation on which a Harvey House was built. Fred Harvey built his houses along railroad routes to service passengers in their travels across

Pottery is fired in hornos or over coals of manure to create a hotter flame. *Library of Congress.*

the country. In the late 1800s, a railroad was built close to the cliff dwellings, which Harvey seized as a perfect opportunity to expand his amenities to more travelers heading west. Contained in the Harvey House are exhibits explaining the discoveries made by Hewett as well as some of the actual artifacts excavated. The Harvey structure is also made from local volcanic tuff to closely resemble the ancient cliff dwellings.

Santa Clara Pueblo, on the west bank of the Rio Grande, is a federally recognized Tewa people. The Indian tribe can trace its ancestors to the Puye Cliff Dwellings and other prehistoric villages west of the current location. The Santa Clara Pueblo is proud to preserve a strong tribal government by instituting a means of providing a solid economy and education system. Their Tewa legacy came under attack as the Spaniards moved into the region and imposed the Spanish way of life and religion on the native peoples. These efforts to convert the native people to Catholicism and suppress the traditional ways that had been observed for centuries created animosity, leading Santa Clara Pueblo to take an active part in the Pueblo Revolt of 1680.

SAN JUAN MISSION CHURCH

A mission was first established as a *visita*, or a chapel, used by a visiting nonresident priest for the San Juan Pueblo in 1628. A permanent residence for the priest was called a *cabacera*. This original church was destroyed by the Tewa tribe to wipe out all Spanish influence from their lands. The structure remained a ruin until the reconquest of 1692, when Don Diego de Vargas returned to Santa Clara and San Ildefonso Pueblos to reestablish control over the native people. Using Black Mesa as a fortress, the Pueblo people stood firm against the Spanish invaders once again until 1696. After this year, they escaped Black Mesa to live with the Hopi and Zuni of western New Mexico. It was not until 1702 that the members of the Santa Clara Pueblo made their way to their homelands once again.

The original church had to be rebuilt multiple times to repair damage inflicted on it by the revolt, but it had completely collapsed by 1750, including the choir loft. Dismayed by these events, Fray Mariano Rodriguez used his

Santa Clara is a small, often forgotten pueblo known for outstanding pottery. *Library of Congress.*

own funds to reconstruct the church in 1758. Beginning the monumental task in the winter, the progress was quite slow, as the people worked on the structure only when they had time, as opposed to being subjected to forced labor by earlier priests.

Although progress was slow, the new structure lasted until 1909, when it was given a modern peaked roof and the vigas were removed from the inside. This proved to be a fatal mistake; the church collapsed as result. A new cruciform church was built in 1918. It is still standing today and is listed with the pueblo in the National Register of Historic Places.

Be sure to obtain a camera permit before photographing the pueblo or the church. For more information concerning this, please call 505-753-7326. Santa Clara Pueblo is open from dawn to dusk.

Santa Clara Pueblo is located on NM 30, two miles south of Española, New Mexico. From US 84/US 285, turn west onto Santa Clara Bridge Road and then turn left heading south on NM 30, also known as the Los Alamos Highway. From NM 30, turn left on to Rose Road and then take a right onto Kee Street, which you will follow to the mission church, which is on the left.

Chapter 8

COCHITI

"Forgotten, or People from the Mountains"
Traditional names: Ko-tyit or K'úutìim'é
Feast day: July 14

Situated between Albuquerque and the capital city of Santa Fe, Cochiti Pueblo contains some of the most unusual landscapes of the nineteen pueblos. For five dollars a carload and a two- to three-hour time investment, you can visit the Kasha-Katuwe National Monument, commonly known as Tent Rocks. There, you will find cone-shaped formations of ash, pumice and tuff deposits from volcanic eruptions that occurred approximately six to seven million years ago. These deposits can be up to one thousand feet thick. Tent Rocks is a must-see during your visit to New Mexico.

As the northernmost Keres-speaking pueblo in New Mexico, Cochiti is home to approximately fifteen hundred people. They are a federally recognized tribe of Native Americans. The pueblo is in the National Register of Historic Places and the New Mexico Register of Cultural Properties and is listed as a United States Historic District. Cochiti Pueblo is officially called K'úutìim'é, which means "People from the Mountains" in Keresan. As descendants of the Anasazi, also known as the Ancient Puebloans, the Cochiti were divided into two groups. The first, Katishtya Pueblo, would later become San Felipe Pueblo. The second, Potrero Viejo Pueblo, was located on a mesa in north-central New Mexico, where they established the temporary pueblo of Hanut Cochiti, which sits about twelve miles northwest of the present-day Cochiti Pueblo. The latter was then moved six miles southeast of the pueblo by Oñate in 1598.

It is thought that the Ancestral Pueblo people moved from the Four Corners region, near present-day Farmington, to establish settlements along the Rio Grande due to drought conditions in AD 1350. Archaeologists refer to this time as the Great Pueblo Migration.

Entrada

As it was with the other pueblos in northern New Mexico, the Entrada of 1598, which saw Spanish conquerors arrive, was a pivotal turning point in the lives of the Puebloan people, and not for the better. As the Spanish colonized the region, the abuse of the native population escalated as the invaders forced the native tribes to do their manual labor while paying taxes of corn and cotton. Restrictions were placed on native ceremonies and rituals, to the point of torture and, in extreme cases, execution. This cruelty led to the Pueblo Revolt of 1680, in which Cochiti Pueblo played an active role.

When the Spanish arrived at the established pueblos, they routinely took over the communities and renamed them after Catholic saints to erase the culture of the native people. Medicine men were often arrested for practicing witchcraft, which led to hangings if convicted. All symbols of the native culture were destroyed, forcing the people to take their rituals underground. It did not bode well for anyone caught practicing the traditions.

Reconquista

Don Diego de Vargas returned to northern New Mexico in the fall of 1692 to reconquer the land for the Spanish Crown. He found San Felipe Pueblo to be friendly at his return. Cochiti Pueblo, on the other hand, remained on the Potrero Viejo Mesa in defiance. De Vargas rallied seventy soldiers, twenty colonists and over one hundred warriors from the pueblos of San Felipe, Santa Ana and Zia to attack Cochiti at midnight. During this attack, de Vargas was able to capture many of the Puebloan people before they were able to flee.

Not deterred by this attack, Cochiti tribal members returned and freed most of the captives, which surprised the Spaniards. De Vargas stayed at the pueblo for a short time before burning it and clearing out the supplies of corn at Potrero Viejo Pueblo to take with him to Santa Fe. Reportedly, more than two hundred women were taken captive to Santa Fe, to be used as servants and slaves or for trade.

After adapting to the Spanish ways a second time, as with other pueblos up and down the Rio Grande, Cochiti residents learned to irrigate their land to plant crops such as maize (corn), beans and calabashes (squash), along with the crops that were introduced to the pueblo people by the Spaniards: wheat, chili peppers, barley, oats, watermelons (sandia), muskmelons (a close relative to the cantaloupe), peaches, pears, apples, grapes, peas, tomatoes and tobacco.

San Buenaventura de Cochiti Mission

Most of the early churches and structures commissioned by the Spanish were crudely built, which meant they usually did not last. Early historical records are nearly nonexistent, but in early 1600, Pueblo de Cochiti became a *visita* of Santo Domingo, and a church was established in 1628 called San Buenaventura de Cochiti Mission.

Bonaventura, an Italian medieval Franciscan scholar and theologian, was one of the greatest philosophers of the Middle Ages. It is reported that he was saved from death as a young man by the prayers of Francis of Assisi. Because of this, Bonaventura spent his time defending the Franciscans from the anti-Mendicant party. It is said that he was instrumental in the election of Pope Gregory X, who rewarded the priest by making him the cardinal bishop of Albano. The priest died in 1274 under suspicious circumstances and was canonized on July 14, 1482. His feast day was originally July 15, but this was the feast of Saint Henry, so it was moved to July 14.

Details about the pre-rebellion church are sketchy, since it was destroyed during the uprising, but in 1706, the mission church was reported to be in poor shape and still in the process of being rebuilt. Cochiti Pueblo residents had taken the iron clapper from the bell of the mission to make tools, mostly likely to be used in agriculture.

In 1760, Bishop Tamerón described Cochiti Pueblo as being less than enthusiastic for the Catholic religion, and the maintenance of the church

San Buenaventura de Cochiti Mission has seen many transformations in its lifetime. *Library of Congress.*

reflected these thoughts. By the late 1770s, Fray Dominguez described San Buenaventura as being "very gloomy," with the church having thick adobe walls, a small belfry over the front entrance, a porter's lodge on the south side, a priest's garden, a corral and a small cemetery in front.

The relationship between the missionaries and the pueblo people was turbulent, with many ups and downs over the years. Prohibition of traditional religious items of the Cochiti was a definite sore spot that never healed. Fray Juan Caballero Toril, the priest for both Cochiti and Santo Domingo Pueblos, strictly prohibited pueblo members from owning any religious item other than Catholic articles, so when he found residents in possession of traditional items, he confiscated and burned them in the center plaza. On the other hand, several years later, Father Noël Dumarest recorded these articles by sketching them for future generations.

When Captain John Gregory Bourke visited Cochiti Pueblo in the 1880s, he observed a church in distress. Rotten ceiling beams, a sagging balcony and holes in the roof were a troubling sight to the captain. He also observed that the pine planks on the whitewashed walls inside of the church were painted with figures of deer, bison, horses and people instead of the expected religious images, which told him that even though Cochiti Pueblo had experienced three hundred years of influence from the Catholic Church, it had not totally given up its traditions and beliefs.

More recently, San Buenaventura de Cochiti Mission has gone through several metamorphoses' since the 1600s. By 1915, unfortunately, the church was in such disrepair that work had to be done quickly to save the historic structure. A pitched tin roof and a twenty-foot-tall steeple were added, while the original wood balcony was removed. The steeple was deemed unsound at that height and was lowered. In the 1960s, through the efforts of Fray Angélico Chávez, leaders of the Cochiti Pueblo and architect Robert Plettenberg, San Buenaventura de Cochiti Mission was returned to its appearance in early images. Today, St. Buenaventura is still an active Catholic parish and was listed in the National Register of Historic Places in 1974, with the Pueblo de Cochiti encompassing 53,779 acres of reservation land.

Although photography and sketching are prohibited, visitors are welcome at San Buenaventura de Cochiti Mission Church.

Arts

Highly valued by native musicians, the ceremonial drums made by the Cochiti Pueblo are most commonly fashioned from hollow wood. Aspen trees are covered by hand-cured leather hides. In 1964, the Storyteller became a popular, profitable art piece for the Pueblo. Pottery is a large market for the Pueblo people, who still use the traditional techniques of their ancestors, while others are branching off to exhibit a more modern take on the art form. Cochiti Pueblo is also known for its painting and printmaking skills. The Montoya, Peña, Herrera and Romero families produce sought-after works of art. In the summer months, tourists will find necklaces made of corn kernels strung on leather straps. These colorful pieces can resemble coral and turquoise and are for purchase at roadside stands.

Nearby Attractions

Kasha-Katuwe National Monument

Between the capital city of Santa Fe and New Mexico's largest city, Albuquerque, is one of the most interesting natural landscapes in the state, Kasha-Katuwe National Monument. You will swear you have entered a

Tent Rocks are alien-like conical formations created from volcanic ash and tuff.

scene out of a Dr. Seuss book as you walk the easy trails through the cone-shaped tent rock formations, which were created from the ash, pumice and tuff deposits of volcanic eruptions six to seven million years ago. These formations, which range from a few feet to 90 feet tall, sit 5,570 to 6,760 feet above sea level and provide great opportunities for birdwatching and studying geology, as well as photography.

Cochiti Lake

Cochiti Lake draws many visitors from around the region to enjoy the facilities located within the boundaries of Pueblo de Cochiti. Sitting at an elevation of 5,343 feet, this beautiful lake is positioned in the foothills of the picturesque Jemez Mountains. Surrounded by juniper and piñon trees, the lake is perfect for windsurfing, paddling and sailing. A five-dollar fee per vehicle will allow you to enjoy all-day fishing, swimming and picnicking. Day use areas are open from April 15 to October 15 every year.

DIRECTIONS: Exit Interstate 25 between Albuquerque and Santa Fe (35 miles southwest) at the Cochiti Pueblo Exit 264– New Mexico 16.

Chapter 9

SALINAS PUEBLO MISSIONS NATIONAL MONUMENT

Salt Mission Pueblos: Abó, Gran Quivira, Quarai

A combination of disease, enemy attacks, weather and lack of water by the 1650s led to all three Salt Missions collectively gaining the moniker "Cities That Died of Fear." The communities were important due to the nearby salt sources at Lake Estañcia. Salt had more value than gold in those times, as it was used for preservation of meat, flavoring and medicinal purposes. Salinas (Salt) Pueblo Missions gained their name from the salt deposits left behind after 150-foot-deep Pleistocene-era lakes evaporated. These deposits were mined and used for trade for centuries by many cultures.

During your visit to the three Salinas Missions, you may encounter more than tourists on the trails. The missions are home to lizards, tarantulas, deer, rabbits, bats and even rattlesnakes, among many others. The rangers ask that, if you encounter any wildlife, please leave them be, since they are protected within the Salinas Pueblo Missions National Monument. The national monument is also proud to host the swearing-in ceremonies of the newest citizens of the United States with music, speeches and dignitaries.

Highly spiritual people, the inhabitants of the Salinas Pueblo Missions, believed that their ancestors came from the five levels of the underground

When walking the pueblo trails, you may encounter other critters on the path. Give them space.

to receive the breath of life from the Corn Mother. This made them an integral part of earth's natural community. As a matriarchal society, it is the clan of the mother, instead of the father, from which the people descend. Women were also the builders of the pueblos; nurturers of the children; joined in on communal hunts; helped to maintain the fields of corn, beans, cotton and squash; and prepared the food for service. The burdens of the women were many, as a lot of responsibility rested on their shoulders. Men were primarily the hunters and farmers, and they produced clothing through working the looms.

Abó

Built by native women and children in the seventeenth century, Abó shows a surprisingly advanced architectural technique for the time. Archaeologists state that when the Spaniards arrived in 1581, they most likely found a thriving community. Fray Francisco Fonte, who was assigned to Abó Mission in 1622, first converted one of the pueblo rooms into a convento before the existence of a church. In this room, he was able to celebrate Mass, perform baptisms and pray.

Records show that a small church and convento were begun in 1623. A curious addition, a circular kiva, was found inside the churches at Abó and Quarai. It was thought that kiva helped in the conversion process when it was completed in 1628. No roofing material was ever found for the kiva, leading rangers and archaeologists to wonder if the Franciscans were initially tolerant of the native traditions, or, since there was trash found in the kiva, if it was desecrated and used as an example against these traditions. It remains a mystery today.

Fray Francisco Acevedo was assigned to Abó in 1629, working for eleven years to convert as many of the Pueblo people as possible by orders of the Spanish Crown. By this time, the first church was in disrepair, so he took it upon himself to begin renovations. The new, larger church was built around the older one so that dismantling of the smaller church could be done, when the time came in 1658, without disturbing services at the new structure.

Livestock was moved from Gran Quivira to Abó for several reasons, including better food and water sources, as well as fewer raids by the Apache in the 1660s. Drought, famine and more brutal raids by the Apache caused the mission to be abandoned in 1673. It stood in silence and ruins until 1815, when a family of sheepherders settled in the area until they were also forced to leave by marauding Apaches in 1830. They were able to permanently return in 1865 after the Apache Wars. Ruins of their red sandstone structures can still be viewed at Abó Pueblo Mission. A magnificent view of the Manzano Mountains can be seen from the Abó ruins, which sit on 370 acres of land, making it one of the most picturesque of the three pueblos.

SAN GREGORIO DE ABÓ MISSION CHURCH

The first sight that greets you when you round the corner on the short road from NM 60 is the thirty-foot red rock towers of San Gregorio de Abó Mission Church reaching to the turquoise sky. Carefully placed sandstone stones measuring no more than one foot in length and four inches in width comprise the outer walls of the mission church. No mortar was used. Instead, loose pebbles and gravel were used as chinks to fill in the spaces. Using this method, it took over half a century, from 1621 to 1673, to complete the church building, with a few years of strife in between.

The nave of San Gregorio de Abó had three stone steps that led up to the three stone altars in the sanctuary of the cross-shaped church. An adobe platform held the central high altar, accessed only by a stairway. Over the years, these high altars have been the target of fortune hunters convinced that the priests buried treasures there before they abandoned the church in the nineteenth and twentieth centuries. Therefore, all that remains of the central high altar is the retaining wall and partial platform.

The original church lines can be seen within the ruins today as stones line the apse wall, which made San Gregorio slightly larger than Mission Nuestra Señora de la Purísima Concepción of Quarai. Renovations between 1640 and 1651 saw the church lengthened, two transepts added and a bell tower moved to the northwest corner of the structure. Priest reports state that in order to ring the bell, a boy would have to first climb into the choir loft, then walk across the convento roof, cross a wooden catwalk over the sanctuary and finally climb the stone stairs to access the rope for the bell.

Today, two wood beams can be seen at the north side of the bell tower. These beams are not original to the first construction but were added during the renovation period. The south-facing clerestory window was supported by these beams. Light from the clerestory window filled the church most

The red rock ruins of Abó Pueblo are a stark contrast to the vivid blue of the New Mexico sky.

San Gregorio Mission Church of Abó features two tall bell towers.

of the day. Although a bit precarious today, the choir loft of San Gregorio housed a "fine organ" in its heyday, and one can only imagine the beautiful quality of acoustics the stone walls provided as the organist played with the accompaniment of trumpets, bells and bassoons.

In the sacristy, where the priest would prepare to say Mass, archaeologist Joseph Toulouse in 1933 found two timbers approximately five feet apart at floor level, which he suspected were parts of a private altar used by the priests for their own devotion. Although the space is void today, it was said to have contained a large wood cabinet used to hold the vestments and vessels for the Mass.

Abandonment of Abó Pueblo

Unable to withstand the constant Apache raids and the severe drought and famine caused by the influx of people who descended on them from the other pueblos, the residents of Abó finally abandoned it in 1672. Many of the residents moved to the Rio Grande Valley, where they did side with the Spaniards during the Pueblo Revolt of 1680.

In 1938, Abó and Quarai Pueblos were lumped in with Gran Quivira when they were purchased by the State of New Mexico as a historic site. The National Parks Service was able to obtain the pueblo sites in 1981, and they are located there today.

By 1912, the railroad had arrived in the region. Ruins that lay next to the tracks officially became a town. Located six miles southwest of Mountainair, New Mexico, Abó had two saloons, a post office, a school and a Catholic church. This would last only until 1940, when the railroad depot was retired. The school closed in 1960.

GRAN QUIVIRA

Gran Quivira is the largest of the Salinas (Salt) Missions, revealed by the discovery of over 226 rooms that were excavated out of one area labeled Mound Seven in the 611-acre site. Thought to have been inhabited by the Jumanos Indians—the same native people who were visited and taught by the "Blue Nun" (see chapter 1)—Gran Quivira is believed to date back to as early as between AD 800 and 1275. The area was also referred to as the Tompiro Pueblos. Gran Quivira was the largest of five villages, with a population of two thousand.

Due to the lack of water sources in the central regions of New Mexico, the Tompiro could not grow crops, so the ability to trade salt for food was vital to the existence of the large pueblo. This commodity made Gran Quivira a major trading hub for other pueblos and the Plains tribes. Fifteen wells, twenty-five feet deep, were dug seven miles west of the pueblo to provide the people with a source of fresh water.

Later occupations would last between the years 1000 and 1600. Explorer Don Antonio de Espejo is thought to have written about the large settlement in his journals in 1583 and was likely the first Spaniard seen by the inhabitants of Las Humanas (Gran Quivira). Don Juan de Oñate arrived in 1598 to colonize New Mexico and visited Las Humanas but decided to move on to the Santa Fe area after he determined there was nothing of value for him there.

A mission was established at Gran Quivira by Fray Alonso de Benavides in 1626 and was not given too much attention until it became a *visita* (satellite mission) of Abó in 1629, the same year construction began on a permanent mission at Gran Quivira. Archaeologists refer to the rooms at the west end of

Mound 7 as Letrado's Convento, after Fray Francisco Letrado, who moved from Zuni Pueblo in 1631 to develop an early chapel and housing for the Spanish settlers. Completion of the mission at Abó was achieved under the supervision of Fray Francisco de Acevedo in 1631.

During the severe drought of the 1660s and 1670s, more than 450 inhabitants of Gran Quivira died from famine and the diseases brought to them by the Spaniards, such as smallpox. In a report from the provincial governor, he wrote, "The wells are exhausted and there is an insufficient water supply for the people, for their lack of water is so great that they are accustomed to saving their urine to water the land and build their walls."

By 1669, Father Juan Bernal observed that the Las Humanas were "lying dead along the roads, in the ravines and in their huts." Through the best efforts of the missionaries who transported tons of grain, beans and livestock for those in need, Apache raids, dangerous roads and the sheer distance made it impossible for them to provide enough support. Approximately 480 people perished in Gran Quivira in just one winter.

Forced to leave their homes and churches and abandon the communities they had developed because of famine, drought, demands from land barons and Apache raiding parties, the Puebloan people never returned. This greatly affected the Apache as well, as the Las Humanas were a primary source of food and slaves. When this source ran dry, the Apache were forced

White ware pottery created by the Jumanos show artistry and talent.

to sell their own people into slavery for food. Many Apache mothers took their babies to the missions so they could survive.

IGLESIA DE SAN ISIDRO MISSION CHURCH

The Iglesia de San Isidro was the earlier of the two churches built at the Gran Quivira site. Thought to have been erected between 1630 and 1635, the church measured 109 feet long and 29 feet wide and was constructed of quarried limestone and placed with mud mortar or caliche. Father Benavides described this chapel as small, even though it was among the widest in the state.

Iglesia de San Isidro's east side had a *campo santo*, which is a walled cemetery attached to a church. As it was Father Letrado's first attempt at building a church, mistakes were made. A miscalculation in weight and structural integrity caused the roof to collapse—the span exceeded the capacity of the beams and load-bearing walls. Pine logs were hauled some twenty miles from the Gallinas Mountains to make the vigas, which were approximately thirty-three feet long. Another structural collapse occurred when the nave was built without transepts, placing added weight on the thin walls of the church structure.

During the 1930s, Gran Quivira, Iglesia de San Isidro became a destination for treasure hunters. They were searching, much like the Spanish conquistadors, for vast lost treasures rumored to have been buried there when the church was abandoned. One was Jacobo Yrisarri, who worked for a decade to excavate a deep shaft in the apse of the church then start a tunnel toward the San Buenaventura Church in search of speculated hoards of gold, silver and diamonds.

SAN BUENAVENTURA DE LAS HUMANAS MISSION CHURCH

Construction of the San Buenaventura Church was begun by Fray Diego de Santander after he was permanently assigned to Gran Quivira in 1659. Before this time, Gran Quivira was raided in the 1650s by the Apaches who destroyed the Iglesia de San Isidro Church and unfortunately were able to capture seventeen women and children to be used as slaves or trade.

Gran Quivira has been the site of extensive treasure hunts.

Fray Santander selected a site to the west of the original San Ysidro mission. Narrower than San Ysidro, at 27 feet wide and 109 feet long, San Buenaventura was built on an east–west axis with the front entrance facing east. It consisted of a full convento and large corrals built south of the church. It is also interesting to note that even though the Las Humanas appeared to embrace the Christian ways on the surface, hidden kivas were found built into the church walls when excavated.

Abandonment of Gran Quivira

Between 1671 and 1672, the culture of Gran Quivira collapsed beyond repair. Surviving community members scattered to other pueblos like Isleta and Abó; others traveled farther south. Unfortunately, because of this mass exodus, the San Buenaventura de Las Humanas Mission Church was never completed, and the hard work of the women was left to languish under the New Mexico sun.

Even one of New Mexico's most notorious outlaws has a connection to Gran Quivira. According to one story, in the spring of 1880, William H.

Bonny (aka "Billy the Kid") and his friend John Meadows were traveling south from Punta de Agua to White Oaks, New Mexico, when they happened upon the ancient remains of the mission at Gran Quivira in their search for water. After exploring an old irrigation ditch, they notice a cross fashioned from cedar on top of the church. Meadows climbed the ruins to the cross and suggested taking it down, but Billy refused, saying, "No, John, it has a history and we'll leave some scientific devil do that."

QUARAI

Rumors of a light-skinned, bearded invader spread through the Salinas Pueblos, sending a degree of fear throughout the communities. When Don Juan de Oñate arrived at Quarai, he was quick to announce that the pueblo was now under the rule of the king of Spain—a person they had never met nor even heard of. The residents would be required to discard much of their way of life for Oñate's benefit. Oñate promised harm and damage to anyone who did not obey the new ruler and his church.

Three years after the Entrada of 1598, warriors from Quarai Pueblo attacked a group of Spaniards who were harvesting salt from Lake Estañcia. Salt from this lake was sacred to the pueblos and served as a source of trade and food preservation. In retaliation for the attack, Oñate sent in his soldiers, who burned the community and killed nine hundred inhabitants. Quarai was also home to three priests who served as the head of the Spanish Inquisition in New Mexico. Spanish settlers were called to Quarai to face charges of superstition, witchcraft, unfaithfulness and blasphemy, among other accusations. Mission residents were not subject to this scrutiny but were often brought in to testify against the accused. Those found guilty were bound and sent to Mexico City for trial.

Work was said to have begun on Mission Nuestra Señora de la Purísima Concepción in 1627. The work was conducted through the skilled efforts of the pueblo women, who were allowed entrance only after completion to cook and make bread. Construction was finished in 1632. One of the most unusual features of the church was the square kiva, constructed within the walls of the structure, much like Abó.

Thought to have been built between 1622 and 1645, the square kiva is an anomaly that has archaeologists scratching their heads. Possibly used as a conversion tool to gain trust of the pueblo inhabitants, the kiva is in the exact center of the convent, much like at Abó. The square shape can

Quarai Pueblo was used as a Spanish homestead.

be traced to the ancestry of the population of the Salinas Missions, which primarily came from the Hopi and Zuni tribes.

Isolation of the site did not bode well for the inhabitants, who became targets of constant raids of the Apache. In addition, severe drought conditions existed, a result of no rain and little water surrounding the mission. Both factors caused famine, disease and the abandonment of the Quarai Pueblo in 1678. Spanish settlers would not return to the area until the 1800s, during which time they built homes, now called the Lucero Structures, on the foundations of the pueblo. In the course of reestablishing a settlement for the second time at Quarai, a *torreon* (round defensive structure made of stone or adobe bricks with cutouts for weapons) was built at the site around 1845 to protect settlers from the raiding parties who still roamed the area.

MISSION NUESTRA SEÑORA DE LA PURÍSIMA CONCEPCIÓN DE QUARAI

Completed in 1632, Mission Nuestra Señora de la Purísima Concepción (Church of the Immaculate Conception) was approved by the Quarai Pueblo in 1626. Fray Alonso de Benavides and Fray Juan Gutierrez de la Chica arrived at the pueblo in 1625 with a supply wagon train from Mexico City; tools, equipment and supplies were sent later. There was reported to be little opposition at Quarai, as opposed to the other pueblos in the region.

Once Gutierrez surveyed the land, he decided to build the church and convento on a mound of ruins in the northeast corner of the pueblo. The church was built in a cruciform (cross) configuration with walls four to five feet thick, some rising to as high as forty feet. The nave (main body) measures one hundred feet long and twenty-seven feet wide. The plans have the transepts measuring fifty feet long and twenty-five feet wide. It remains the most complete of the three Salinas Pueblo Missions. If you look closely, you will be able to see the fingerprints and handprints of the ancient builders embedded in the mortar.

During a military expedition in the winter of 1853, Major James H. Carleton visited Quarai and Abó and reportedly was surprised to find the ruins in a state of good preservation for their age. Quarai is the most complete of the three missions. In his report, Carleton stated about Abó: "The tall ruins standing there in solitude, had an aspect of sadness and

Mission Nuestra Señora de la Purísima Concepción de Quarai.

gloom. The cold wind seemed to roar and howl through the roofless pile like an angry demon."

While being treated to a guided personal tour of Quarai by park ranger, childhood friend and classmate Murt Sullivan, we were given a wonderful gift. Standing in a doorway, trying to get out of a small rain shower that was passing over, we heard an angelic voice rise from the sanctuary, singing the hymn "Amazing Grace." A young girl in her late teens had been so moved by the setting that she was prompted to spontaneously express it in song. Goosebumps and tears ensued, an amazing spiritual experience I will never forget.

Chapter 10

ZUNI

A'Shiwi, or "The flesh"
Traditional name: Halona, Itiwan'a ("Middle Place"), She-we-na
Pronounciation: ZOON-yee

The surrounding nature at Zuni Pueblo has been an inspiration to the Zuni people for thousands of years. The Zuni culture is based on a matrilineal clan system highly laden with ceremony and ritual firmly centered on the beliefs of the ancestors, or ancient ones. The farming society, comprising nearly twelve thousand people, raises wheat and maize (corn) to sustain it, much like ancestors did throughout the ages.

The Zuni used ingenious "waffle" gardens, which consisted of sunken squares that would aid in the capture of runoff water. This method allowed the Zuni to survive in the arid landscape—one of the oldest continually cultivated areas in the United States. Waffle gardens are still used by the Zuni and in other regions today.

Located approximately 150 miles west of New Mexico's largest city, Albuquerque, Zuni Pueblo is centrally located enough to afford its residents any amenity necessary but still adequately remote to ensure the preservation of the 450,000-acre ancient culture, which also stretches into the state of Arizona. In the 1600s, an assignment to Zuni by the church was seen by a priest as punishment. One priest, learning of his fate, wrote, "If it had been chosen for a prison for those guilty of the gravest crimes there would have not been a more severe decision."

In February 1632, Zuni warriors ambushed Father Francisco de Letrado at the mission and killed him. Within five days, another priest was killed and the mission burned. After these deeds, the warriors fled to Dowa Yalanne (Corn Mesa, sometimes called Thunder Mountain) fearing retaliation from the Spanish.

Zuni Pueblo sits in the shadow of Dowa Yalanne, a steep mesa approximately three and a half miles from the pueblo. The mesa includes a shrine cave near the top. The Zuni Pueblo is one of the oldest continuously inhabited settlements in the United States, established since at least AD 1100. Missionary contact did not begin until 1629.

Due to their remoteness, the Zuni people speak a language unique to them, Shiwi'ma, said to be a "highly literal and descriptive language" that uses a variety of compound words. The Zuni are known for their jewelry-making skills as well as for baskets, beadwork, pottery and carved-animal fetishes. Although many today have embraced the modern way of life, they keep the ancient traditions alive.

Most pueblos have a distinct form of artwork that sets them apart from the rest. In Zuni's case, it is the carving of stone fetishes. The Zuni people also are known for their paintings, jewelry and pottery. Zuni history is marked by the use of painted pottery and carved fetishes to record the stories of the past, since the written word is rarely used in native culture. Enchanting red sandstone mesas rising nearly eight thousand feet on the western slope of the Continental Divide encompass the pueblo, providing a great source of inspiration and materials for the native artists.

Seven Cities of Cibola

In 1539, Estevanico Estebanico, or Esteban, as he is better known, whose real name was Mustafa Azemmouri, of Arab/Barbary or Moroccan (Moor) descent, became a part of the early exploration of New Mexico. After returning to Mexico after a Florida expedition, he came to the new land in search of the "Seven Cities of Cibola," or the "Seven Cities of Gold" fabled lands of riches and gold, which the Spanish Crown desperately needed. Esteban traveled up from Mexico as a scout two weeks ahead of Franciscan friar Marcos De Niza.

Esteban, the first African explorer of North America and called "the first great African man in America," was sold into slavery in 1522 in Azemmour, a Portuguese-controlled town on Morocco's Atlantic coast. The ill-fated Andres Dorantes de Carranza from Spain acquired the services of Esteban as a servant. Carranza was an explorer and had traveled to the Americas for personal enrichment. Since Spain would not allow anyone not of the Catholic faith to journey to the New World, Esteban, who may have been raised Muslim, most likely converted to Catholicism to be able to take the trek with Carranza.

In 1527, Dorantes and Esteban traveled to Florida, where they were met with a hurricane and resistance from the native tribes in the area, which caused the deaths of many in their expedition. After they decided to leave Florida, three of their ships sank on the way to Mexico. With only eighty survivors, the group had to make land in the area of present-day Galveston, where the harsh winter and lack of supplies reduced the group to just fifteen members, three of whom were Dorantes, Esteban and Southwest explorer Cabeza de Vaca. The ragtag group of men wandered nearly two thousand miles on foot throughout Texas and into New Mexico for eight years, during which they were often enslaved by local native tribes. They finally arrived in Mexico in 1536. Dorantes was offered a new expedition, but after his harrowing experiences, he refused. He sold Estevanico to the viceroy of New Spain, Antonio de Mendoza, and attempted to return to Spain. But after his ship was judged unfit to sail, he was forced to return to Veracruz, Mexico, never to leave.

Due to his eight-year journey in the Southwest and his association with Cabeza de Vaca, the viceroy chose Esteban to serve as a guide for a new expedition into New Spain in 1539 to find the rumored lost cities of gold with Friar Niza. It is said that Niza was traveling too slow for Esteban's liking, so Esteban forged on ahead by a few days with a plan to send a cross back to the friar of a size that correlated with the news or treasures found. Small crosses were sent back generally, except for the one reportedly "the size of a man" from Hawikuh, near the Zuni Pueblo area. Friar Niza was excited by the possibilities and decided to break camp to join Esteban farther north.

Before the priest could travel very far, word came back of Esteban's untimely death. Speculation about the cause of his death has existed for centuries. Some say it was due to the fact that he was of African descent, probably the first encountered by the Zuni people. Esteban was allegedly wearing owl feathers and carrying a medicine gourd, which was interpreted by the Zuni as Esteban pretending to be a medicine man, a deed punishable by death. Some have theorized that he displayed cruelty by demanding turquoise and women, or that he faked his death in order to get out from under the Spaniard's ownership as a slave. According to legend, Chakwaina, the kachina figure carved by the natives, is a black kachina, said to reflect their encounter with Esteban.

No matter the reason, Friar Niza returned to Mexico with elaborate stories of great treasures in the city of Cibola to justify the expense of the expedition. This enticed Francisco Vázquez de Coronado to be the next to travel north. Coronado was soon to find out, in 1540, that the good priest and Alva Nunez Cabeza de Vaca were not always truthful in their storytelling.

A starving Coronado and his army of nearly two thousand men arrived at the famed town of Cibola in July 1540, only to be bitterly disappointed by what they found—or, more accurately, what they did not find. After demanding food and shelter, wiping out the supplies of the native inhabitants, creating havoc and facilitating the deaths of nearly the entire tribe, Coronado moved on to the Tiguex nation to repeat the scenario. The Zuni Pueblo residents were left to pick up the pieces and rebuild their life.

Nuestra Señora de Guadalupe

Located at Halona Pueblo, the original name of the Zuni Pueblo, this beautiful church is said to be an excellent example of early Spanish Colonial architecture and dates to 1629. The date is controversial, however, since the Halona Pueblo is not mentioned in text until AD 1663. The mission church is referred to as Nuestra Señora de la Candelaria de Halona in this reference, but it is agreed that Nuestra Señora de Guadalupe Mission (Our Lady of Guadalupe Mission) Church was one of three missions established by Franciscan friars assigned to the region by Don Juan de Oñate. La Purísima Concepción de Hawikuh and the church at Kechipan near Ojo Caliente (never completed) are the other two missions also on the Zuni Reservation.

After the head priest in Santa Fe ordered all the religious items of the indigenous people destroyed in 1645, the Navajo and Jemez planned a revolt. After the first Spaniard was killed, the military executed twenty-nine villagers, publically whipped many others and sold women and children into slavery. Another uprising in 1650 resulted in the hanging of nine men, with even more sold into slavery.

An enclosed adobe convento was the original mission; it was burned during the Pueblo Revolt of 1680, when the priest was also killed. The

Zuni Pueblo Mission Church before restoration. *Library of Congress.*

people of Zuni Pueblo fled to a village on Dowa Yalanne (Corn Mesa), where they remained during the revolt and attacks by the Apache until the Spaniards returned in 1692. By 1699, the Zuni people had returned to the site to participate in the rebuilding of the church in 1705 and then again in 1780.

Of adobe brick construction, the church was constantly maintained by the Zuni people, who also added two bell towers and a balcony. When Mexico won its independence from Spain in 1821, the Franciscan priests left the mission without replacements. As a result, the church fell into poor condition and remained that way until the priests returned in 1921.

The twentieth century saw the church receive many repairs, including a new roof in 1905 and major renovations in the 1960s, leading to the reconstruction of the church. Today, murals depicting the ancient traditions of the Zuni Pueblo kachinas have been painted inside the former Catholic church by Zuni artist Alex Seowtewa. The church and pueblo are listed in the National Register of Historic Places. The site comprises the church, plaza, homes, hornos and waffle gardens. It is unfortunate that the church

Zuni Pueblo Mission Church after restoration. *Library of Congress.*

is now in desperate need of preservation as a result of being unused. This treasure is literally crumbling away.

Photography is allowed by permission only. Please check with the Zuni Pueblo Department of Tourism to gain access to the church. Tours are available for a fee, and reservations can be made by contacting the visitor center at 505-782-7238. They suggest a week's advance notice.

Chapter II

ACOMA

"Place That Always Was"
Traditional name: Haak'u
Feast day: First Sunday in May

Perched on a mesa high above the desert floor is Acoma Pueblo, also known as Sky City. The inhabitants carry on the tradition of speaking their ancient language of Keresan as well as English. Acoma Pueblo is considered the oldest continuously inhabited community in the United States and looks very much like it did in ancient times. Tours are available, allowing visitors to see and experience the ancient ways of life that are still in place on top of the mesa. Residents of the stunningly beautiful pueblo have chosen to adhere to the old ways by living without electricity or running water. As was done in days gone by, dwellers must make the trek down the mesa on foot to obtain water for their daily use, as vehicles cannot access the Sky City. All materials used to build Acoma Pueblo were carried up the steep mesa on the residents' backs.

To provide sustenance to its people, Acoma Pueblo raised five varieties of corn—each a different color—as well as gourds to use for water vessels and rattles, as well as cotton for trade textiles. The Spanish brought with them other crops, which were integrated into the lifestyle, some with a less than wholehearted response. Wheat was raised but not truly accepted, but a variety of fruit, including pears, grapes, apricots, apples and peaches, was embraced. The chili pepper was also introduced by the Spaniards, and it has become a mainstay ingredient of the New Mexican diet.

Known as Sky City, Acoma Pueblo is 365 feet above the desert floor. *Library of Congress.*

After the Entrada of 1598 by Don Juan de Oñate, an attempt was made to incorporate the Puebloan people into the Spanish Empire as he gathered representatives from the pueblos. Acoma was one of the last to take the oath of allegiance to the Spaniards. Although most of the pueblos stated a willingness to accept the ways of the Spaniards and their god, it was thought that most did not completely understand the connotations of what Oñate was saying due to the language barriers. The natives may not have understood that failure to accept the demands of the invaders could have deadly consequences.

In November 1598, after the Oñate party had left, Juan de Zaldivar, Oñate's *maese de campo* (controller of stores) and nephew, arrived at Acoma with a small group. Appearing peaceful, the inhabitants of Acoma accepted their arrival, but when Zaldivar demanded most of the pueblo's remaining stored food items for his group, the pueblo attacked, killing most of the party.

Chief Zuta-Kapan was said to have killed Zaldivar with a club, while the other warriors took care of the twelve soldiers and two slaves. To escape the brutality, five soldiers jumped from the top of the mesa; one was killed, and the others were injured. It was these soldiers who alerted Oñate of the attack.

Juan's brother, Vicente de Zaldivar, was sent to avenge the death with seventy men. The Spaniards made three attempts to have the pueblo surrender peacefully, but all failed. Soldiers scaled the mesa walls to begin a two-day battle, in which only six hundred of the reported three thousand inhabitants of Acoma survived. Oñate reported to the Crown: "As punishment for its crime and its treason against his Majesty, to whom it had already rendered submission by a public instrument, and as a warning to the rest, I razed and burned it completely, in the way in which your Lordship will see by the process of this cause."

This action is disputed by the records of the Acoma Pueblo and archaeological sources. It is said that there is evidence that surrounding pueblos other than Acoma were destroyed by the Spanish by mistake. The ruins, within a radius of fifteen to twenty miles, indicate that the site was destroyed by means other than natural degradation. Acoma remained untouched by fire but met the wrath of Oñate, who tried the inhabitants of Acoma for treason as Spanish subjects.

After the trial in February 1599, it was determined that treason was committed, and sentences must be carried out immediately. It was the order of Oñate that all men and women over the age of twelve be sentenced to twenty years of servitude (slavery). As further punishment, half of the right feet of men over the age of twenty-five was to be cut off—especially devastating, since the pueblo is atop a high mesa and hunting would be nearly impossible for those men. In fact, the Acoma men were great runners. Children under the age of twelve were said to be free, but sixty girls were sent to convents in Mexico, and the boys were given to Vincente de Zaldivar as military slaves. The elderly people met a poor fate as well, given to a sworn enemy of the pueblo people, the Apache, for care. These atrocities would be known as the 1599 Acoma Massacre.

A statue of Don Juan de Oñate was erected in Alcalde, New Mexico, much to the dismay of the surrounding pueblos. It was mysteriously relieved of its right foot from time to time before it was taken down in 2020. Acoma was said to have been rebuilt between the years 1629 and 1640 by the men and women who returned home after their twenty-year servitude sentence. Fray Ramirez took credit for showing them how to construct homes from wood and adobe.

SAN ESTEBAN REY MISSION CHURCH

During the reconstruction at Acoma Pueblo, San Esteban Rey (Saint Stephen the King) Mission Church was built under the instruction of Fray Ramirez, who had established himself at the pueblo to affect change. It was said that in 1634, the priest was able to convince the pueblo people of the value of baptism by baptizing a child who was said to have been "bewitched by a sorcerer" and that, by doing so, the child immediately became well. Seeing this convinced the pueblo people of the power of baptism and of the words being preached to them, making conversion an easier task for the priest.

Construction of San Esteban Rey Mission Church took twelve years to complete, from 1629 to 1642. Measuring 150 feet long and 40 feet wide, the adobe-and-plaster church featured an adobe roof over wood vigas, which were 40 feet long and 14 inches square. The San Mateo Mountains, thirty miles away, provided the lumber to finish construction of the church.

Seven-foot-thick adobe walls grace one side of the church, while five-foot-thick walls support the other side with a parapet and square twin tower belfries, which face east, a Pueblo tradition. Whitewash covers the

The only access to Acoma Pueblo is a narrow footpath. *Library of Congress.*

interior of the sparsely decorated church, and there is a choir loft above the entrance. Every resident, young and old, was employed by the Franciscans to build the church and convento. San Esteban del Rey Mission Church is now a National Historic Landmark and is documented by the National Park Service's Historic American Buildings Survey.

The Spanish continued with their methods of force to instill their ways on the Pueblo people, but limits were placed on the forms of punishment meted out. For instance, cutting off hair for minor infractions was outlawed. Some members of the pueblo conformed; others plotted the Pueblo Revolt of 1680, in which the resident priest was killed. The church survived. Acoma was again attacked in 1696 by Don Diego de Vargas, but his attempt was foiled, and the plan failed.

ACOMA TODAY

Each pueblo has its own traditions and talents. As with many of the other communities, Acoma is known for its exquisite pottery making. The fine-walled polychrome pottery with intricate geometric painted designs formed from native clays has become a staple in the continuing economy of the

Tours are available to view present-day Acoma Pueblo via permit only. *Library of Congress.*

pueblo, as the vessels are highly prized and collected worldwide. Guided tours of the pueblo and church are available for a fee. Photography is allowed of the pueblo with a permit, but it is asked that no images of the cemetery or interior of the church be taken. Please be respectful of the residents and the rules. The pueblo is their permanent home.

Chapter 12

LAGUNA

"Small Lake"
Traditional name: Ka'waika, Kawaik
Pronunciation: Lah-GOO-nah
Feast days: March 19 (Old Laguna), July 26 (Seama Village), August 15 (Mesita Village), September 8 (Encinal), September 19 (Laguna), September 25 (Laguna), October 17 (Village of Paraje)

Archaeologists believe the part of New Mexico where Laguna Pueblo now stands was inhabited by ancient people over ten thousand years ago. The relatives of the Laguna people thrived in the Rio Grande Basin along the San Jose River beginning in 3000 BCE. There, they grew life-sustaining dominant crops of maize, beans and squash by using early irrigation methods from the Arroyo de Rito (Brook of the Spring), more popularly known later as the San Jose River. The entire pueblo spans four counties and includes the communities of Laguna, Mesita, Peguate, Seama, Encinal and Paraje on five hundred thousand acres of land.

Laguna Pueblo inhabitants spoke Keresan. Laguna is the largest of the Keresan pueblos, at 108 acres. It was listed in the National Register of Historic Places in 1973. Known as the Kawaik people among their own, the population's name was changed by the Spanish to Laguna, due to the pueblo's proximity to a local lake. The Kawaik were in a good central location along the San Juan River between the Ancestral Pueblo people near present-day Aztec and the Mogollon people to the south near today's Silver

City. The self-governing agricultural community astounded the Spanish when they arrived in the early 1500s, and the residents were quickly put to work for the benefit of the Spaniards.

SAN JOSÉ DE LAGUNA MISSION CHURCH

The whitewashed plastered exterior adobe walls of San José de Laguna Mission Church are visible for miles around as it sits perched high above the pueblo community of Laguna. Constructed in 1699, primarily from adobe and fieldstone, San José de Laguna Mission Church is dedicated to Saint Joseph and boasts an artful interior. Colorful retablos (devotional images) painted on a carved wooden altar screen with spiral pillars grace the wall behind the altar, a highly unique seventeenth-century painting done on buffalo hide, and rare Spanish paintings grace the inner sanctum of the small church. Murals of tribal symbols in vivid shades of green, red, black, terra cotta and yellow painted by Laguna Pueblo members ring the interior at chair-rail height. The whitewashed interior walls truly blend the two cultures represented (native and Hispanic) through art.

PAINTING OF SAN JOSÉ

A painting of San José (Saint Joseph) holding the Christ child was brought to neighboring Acoma Pueblo by Franciscan Friar Ramirez, who received the artwork directly from King Charles II. Both Acoma and Laguna Pueblos soon began to believe the painting held supernatural powers, as Acoma Pueblo began to flourish with added rain after its arrival. Laguna was in drought situations. In an effort to save Laguna, the pueblo leaders asked Acoma to share the painting so they could also have the good fortune of rain. The people of Acoma were not keen on the idea and suggested they draw lots to let God decide after a yearlong stalemate.

When the results determined that the painting remain at Acoma, the Laguna people, incensed with the negative results, broke into the Acoma church and stole the painting. Fury spread through Acoma, but somehow, Father Ramirez was able to calm the people down and convince them to lend the artwork to Laguna for a short time. When the painting's reputation

The interior of San José de Laguna Mission Church is decorated with buffalo hides. *Library of Congress.*

worked at Laguna as well and that pueblo began to flourish, its residents refused to return it to the Acoma Pueblo. This battle raged on for over a century before Acoma finally filed a lawsuit against Laguna in the Supreme Court of New Mexico.

The court ruled that the painting belonged to Acoma Pueblo and must be returned. Legend states that the painting was found resting against a mesquite tree in a canyon separating the two pueblos by members of the Acoma Pueblo charged with retrieving the sacred art. Acoma Pueblo lore states, "The Saint was in such a hurry to return home to Acoma, that he started out on his own."

The church building, east and slightly north of the town of Grants and forty-five miles west of Albuquerque, is visible from Interstate 40. It served as a stable for the natives during the Pueblo Revolt of 1680. It was repaired in the 1930s and restored into a place of worship.

Route 66, or the "Mother Road," and Interstate 40 cut a swath through pueblo lands. This road brought many tourists to the Laguna Pueblo area, giving pueblo artisans an excellent chance to sell their outstanding pottery. Before 1937, Route 66 was a large *S*-shaped highway in New Mexico, but with the decision to straighten it out in 1926, Route 66 was aligned through the town of Santa Fe along the old Santa Fe–Las Vegas loop. In 1937, it

San José de Laguna Mission Church of Laguna Pueblo is visible from Interstate 40. *Library of Congress.*

was realigned farther south, when the "Santa Fe cut-off" shortened the road, which took an east–west course from Santa Rosa through Moriarty to Albuquerque, bypassing Santa Fe and Los Lunas. Although cutting the miles from 506 to 399, Laguna Pueblo was still included along the route.

Uranium was discovered on Laguna Pueblo land in the 1950s, and this became a huge economic boost for the small village. Today, the main economic provider is the Route 66 Tribal Casino along Interstate 40 near Albuquerque. Tourism also helps to sustain the pueblo.

Laguna Pueblo sits on 500,000 acres of reservation land along the Rio San José in the foothills of Mount Taylor and comprises four New Mexico counties—Bernalillo, Sandoval, Cibola and Valencia. The laguna for which the pueblo is named was much larger in past times, but it now is still home to large flocks of ducks, geese and swans.

Photography is limited to designated areas. Admission to Laguna Pueblo is free.

Chapter 13

TESUQUE

"Cottonwood Tree Place"
Traditional name: Tet-Sugeh
Feast day: November 12

As one of the least-known pueblos in the group, Tesuque Pueblo is best known as the site of the natural rock formation called Camel Rock. It is also home to several celebrities, such as actress Ali MacGraw and actors Val Kilmer and Ted Danson. On Interstate 25 north between Santa Fe and Taos, Tesuque is in a striking setting with piñon and juniper trees dotting the landscape. Adobe homes can be seen scattered throughout the hillsides.

The Tesuque tribe has lived in this area since the 1200s and was one of the first to build a pueblo in the area. As it was a small pueblo, the residents generally kept to themselves, even after the Spanish Entrada of 1598. Since their home was surrounded by Hispanic farms and settlements, Tesuque Pueblo blended in well with its surroundings, but this did not free the residents from falling victim to the same ill treatment received in neighboring villages. As with the other pueblos in the region, this poor treatment was the reason for the planning of the Pueblo Revolt in 1680.

Secret plans were developed in Tesuque that depended on the complete trust of all inhabitants, but this was betrayed by two Indians, Catua and Omtua, who informed the Spanish officials of the scheme. When their disloyalty was discovered, messengers were sent to all the other pueblos to

Camel Rock near Tesuque Pueblo is a natural sandstone formation.

move up the revolt. The first attack was at night at Tesuque Pueblo, when Cristobal de Herrera was killed. Reverend Padre Juan Bautista Pio, traveling to say Mass at the pueblo, and a soldier named Pedro Hidalgo were attacked the next morning.

The two were greeted by armed warriors from Tesuque and Cuyamangue covered in war paint. When the priest questioned the reasons behind the "savage" look, he was forced into a ravine, where he was slain. Hidalgo was able to thwart the attack and escape. Pio's name was placed at the top of the list of martyrs of the Pueblo Revolt. Dr. Isidro Sariñana y Cuenca, an orator of the Seraphic Order, stated, "If confederated cruelty was wickedly pursuing innocence, it is clear that there had to be a Pio as the first target of arrows which infidelity and apostasy shot against the Christian religion."

SAN DIEGO DE TESUQUE MISSION CHURCH

By 1610, after the Entrada of Don Juan de Oñate, a small church had been fashioned at Tesuque Pueblo. First dedicated under the name San Lorenzo de Alcala de Tesuque, then San Lorenzo de Tesuque Mission and finally

Tesuque Pueblo, the mission church was founded by Father Alonso de Benavides in the 1620s.

The feast day of Saint Lorenzo is August 10, which coincidently is the same day as the Pueblo Revolt. The church served the community until being destroyed in the Pueblo Revolt of 1680. Another church would not be constructed until 1695, after Don Diego de Vargas returned to the area. The new church, built by Fray José Díez, was named San Diego, perhaps due to the negative connotations with the pervious saint's day. This structure would survive the Rebellion of 1696, mainly due to the fact that the Tesuque people were loyal to Diego de Vargas.

Unfortunately, the small church was described as deteriorated by the missionary at Nambé, Fray Francisco de la Concepción Gonzalez, in 1745. Gonzalez had a hostile relationship with Governor Gaspar Domingo de Mendoza, generally over the use of native labor. Located just to the side of the town plaza, sitting in an east–west configuration, San Diego de Tesuque Mission Church seemed to be in constant need of repair, as its

Corn, a food staple of the pueblos, is ground by hand with a mano and matate. *Library of Congress.*

plaster was cracked and peeling, so described in most of the reports written about the structure.

This structure was described in 1777 as measuring about eighty-five feet long by twenty feet wide with a ceiling height of twenty-two feet, having no choir loft, which was thought to mean there was a lack of interest in the Christians' music at the pueblo. Thirty hand-carved log beams stretched across the ceiling and rested on small corbels, which, even when new, appeared to be precarious. Built in a modified cruciform shape, San Diego de Tesuque had a dirt floor, as was the custom.

San Diego de Tesuque would remain a visita of Santa Fe until the end of the eighteenth century, when the population of Tesuque Pueblo began to dwindle. It was at that time that a priest was not needed in residence; one was dispatched from nearby Nambé to say Mass, although it was reported that a priest was in residence between 1729 and 1772. Catechism was assigned to a fiscal mayor of the tribe, who was appointed to assist the priest on Saturdays and feast days to recite the rosary, but a priest would travel from Nambé to hear confessions. Due to its configuration in the community, some believe the church was not completely accepted by the native culture.

Chapter 14

POJOAQUE

"Water Gathering Place"
Traditional name: Po-Suwae-Geh
Feast day: December 12

Settled about AD 500, Pojoaque Pueblo had its largest population numbers between the fifteenth and sixteenth centuries. The Tewa-speaking pueblo faced a devastating smallpox epidemic in 1900 that caused the settlement to be abandoned by the time of New Mexico's statehood in 1912. But it was not federally recognized as an Indian reservation until 1936, two years after it had been repopulated.

With a population of only one hundred in 1707, Pojoaque Pueblo was located sixteen miles north of Santa Fe and three miles from the Nambé Pueblo. The first mention of the Nuestra Señora de Guadalupe de Pojoaque Church was in 1765, when it shows up in a report by Fray Jose Esparragoza y Adame of Nambé, who initiated work on the structure. After Fray y Adame was transferred, the work was completed in 1773 by Fray Juan Jose Llanos.

Nuestra Señora de Guadalupe de Pojoaque Mission Church

Although it was good to have the mission church completed, the quality of work was questionable, as repairs had to be made on the structure in

Pojoaque Pueblo, circa 1850. *Library of Congress.*

1804. Father Dominguez wrote that the church was "carelessly wrought" and had "badly laid beams." The Ortiz family, the major landowners in Pojoaque, paid for the repairs to the sanctuary and commissioned an altar screen depicting Our Lady of Guadalupe. The church was declared "good and new" by Fray Diego Martinez Ramirez de Arellano in 1706, one month before Don Antonio Jose Ortiz died.

When Lieutenant John Bourke visited Pojoaque Pueblo in 1881, he made these observations:

> *This pueblo, so to call it, of Pojuaque* [sic] *is very dilapidated.... Visited the old church, alongside of which are the ruins of the convent, formerly standing here. Within bowshot, is the orchard and vineyard of the pueblo and here growing in full luxuriance were apples, pears, peaches, apricots, plums, grapes, and different kinds of vegetables. The inhabitants of Pojuaque [*sic*] differ in no essential from the Mexicans surrounding them. The church, in its interior, is one of the most thoroughly archaic in all New Mexico. Upon the walls are numerous paintings of saints, some of which manifest an improvement in artistic taste and skill over those I've seen elsewhere. There are several which, if properly cleaned, would be, I think, very beautiful, notably that of Our Lady of Guadalupe, over the main altar.*

A human skull, typical of Life's destiny, surmounts the old Confessional. These very good pictures bore every sign of having come from Spain; others, I've no doubt, came from Mexico, the ruder sketches in the panels of the altar piece, in all probability were the work of the Indians themselves.

One of the pictures is so blackened by age and a deposit of soot that its subject cannot be distinguished. Near the altar, is a crucifix, whereon hangs Our Savior, his body raw with crimson wounds and in attendance upon him a decidedly dumpy little angel.

A pitched, three-sectioned roof and a schoolhouse cupola were applied in approximately 1906 or 1907, when it was popular to "modernize" the mission churches to preserve them. This practice took away the integrity of the adobe structures and distracted from the original design. Many of the churches chose to remove the metal roofs in the future and replaced the traditional flat surfaces with latillas and beamed coverings.

Today, Pojoaque Pueblo is one of the largest employers along I-25, with its Buffalo Thunder Casino and Poeh (Pathway) Center. Buffalo Thunder Casino has a collection of three hundred pieces of Native American sculpture, representing every native tribe in New Mexico.

Poeh Cultural Center is a good representation of how Pojoaque Pueblo once appeared.

Chapter 15

SAN FELIPE

Traditional name: Katishtya
Feast day: May 1

At the foot of the imposing Black Mesa, Katishtya, or the San Felipe Pueblo, is home to a population of nearly 3,400 souls, according to the 2010 Census. The Rio Grande provides the lifeblood for the community as it meanders through the picturesque valley close to the San Felipe volcanic field of the Santa Ana Mesa. Most of the streets are still dirt, and the site could, without the presence of vehicles and modern conveniences, be mistaken for the original pueblo. Encompassing 68,000 acres between the two large population centers of Albuquerque and Santa Fe, San Felipe Pueblo's residents are proud to be known as passionate about preserving their traditions and culture.

The native language of the pueblo, Keresan, is proudly still taught to the up-and-coming generations, who are thought to have descended, as with all the other Pueblo people, from the Anasazi. First contact with the Spanish may have been with the visitation of Francisco Vázquez de Coronado in 1540. San Felipe gained its name in 1591, when Spanish explorer Gaspar Castaño de Sosa, a known slaver and fugitive of the Spanish Crown, visited the pueblo and reportedly named it after a Jesuit priest who was martyred in Japan. Over four hundred priests were martyred for their faith in Japan from the 1540s to 1639, many executed by crucifixion, slow burning at the stake or by means of the pit torture. Of the four hundred, forty-two have been canonized as saints.

When Don Juan de Oñate arrived in 1598, it is said he found a pueblo on the east and west side of the Rio Grande at San Felipe. The Spanish introduced the natives to the new crops of peaches, peppers and wheat they had brought with them. It was Oñate who carried on the process of subjugation of the local tribe. The people were forced to pay taxes to the Spanish Crown in the form of crops, cotton/wool and labor. Pueblo religion and practices were outlawed and forbidden under the penalty of death should anyone be caught.

During the Pueblo Revolt of 1680, the Spaniards were driven from the lands of northern New Mexico, and the church was ransacked by the natives. No Spanish were killed at San Felipe Pueblo; they were able to get to Isleta Pueblo unharmed. In 1681, some Spanish explorers returned to the pueblo, finding it abandoned. They proceeded to loot and burn the structures. The people of San Felipe Pueblo had fled to the top of Horn Mesa (near Cochiti Pueblo, where San Felipe residents had lived for a time before splitting ahead of the Spanish arrival) to protect themselves in just such a situation.

A few Spaniards returned in 1692 under the leadership of Don Diego de Vargas, who was charged in a reconquest campaign against which many of the pueblos also fought. San Felipe was one of the few pueblos that sided with Vargas, alienating it from its neighbors. The pueblo decided, with much coaxing from the Spanish, to be baptized. Residents moved from Horn Mesa to the top of Santa Ana Mesa, where they remained until 1696. It was after they descended from the mesa that they rebuilt the modern pueblo, where it stands today. Today's San Felipe Pueblo continues to be private, with little mingling with those nearby.

Today, approximately 3,200 people live in the small village. During the Feast Day of San Felipe (May 1), Pueblo people perform the Corn Dance, which involves the entire population. By the end of the day, the ground at the plaza is so worn from the amount of dancing done by hundreds of participants that it is bowl-shaped. Although the public can enter the pueblo, very few shops are open or amenities available during most of the year. The best time to visit is when the pueblo has its annual arts and crafts show, generally held in October. Traditional foods, jewelry, crafts and dancing can be experienced by the public during the yearly art show.

For those who like to take their chances at the gaming tables, San Felipe Pueblo owns and operates the Black Mesa Casino on Interstate 25 between Albuquerque and Santa Fe. A tribal-run gas station, restaurant, gift shop and motor sports track are also available across from the casino itself.

Although the ancient village offers many photo opportunities as one navigates the dirt roads that spider through it, one must resist the temptation to snap a few shots, San Felipe Pueblo has a "no photo, sketching, camcorders or audio recording" policy. A sign at the church states that violating this rule can cost the offender $5,000 and the confiscation of all equipment, including cellphones, cameras and recording devices. Remember, these are private homes.

SAN FELIPE MISSION CHURCH

The first mission church was built in the eastern village of San Felipe between 1629 and 1630 by Franciscan friar Juan de Salas. During the Pueblo Revolt of 1680, the people of San Felipe retreated to Santa Ana Mesa, and the Spanish did not feel completely safe coming back into the area until the early 1700s, after the Revolt of 1696 had been quelled. Spanish explorer Diego de Vargas coaxed the Pueblo people from their mesa stronghold to rebuild the pueblo and mission church in the year 1700. The new San Felipe Mission Church was completed in 1736 on the site of the destroyed church, of which Fray Juan Àlvarez had written in his 1706 report to Spain. The original was built in 1598 but burned during the Pueblo Revolt of 1680. The rebuilt church now serves as the centerpiece of the pueblo. No access to the church or churchyard is allowed to the non-Puebloan public either physically or by means of photography. A hefty fine of $2,000 is possible for violators of the rules.

In the summer of 1743, the convento was described by Fray Pedro Montaño as being "full of holes and almost gone." The building was being used as a stable and was full of manure and dirt, with no doors and a dilapidated roof. The priest provided new doors, cleaned out the sanctuary and put in new windows in a little over three months. This rebuilding did not greatly transform the appearance of the church at that time. Located less than one hundred yards south of San Felipe's main plaza, the church faces east toward the river.

When the San Felipe Mission Church was rebuilt in 1808, it featured two buttressed bell towers, a roofed balcony over the front door and a large statue of St. Philip the Apostle. Inside, a new altar was fashioned with a wood, hand-painted altar screen fit to the back wall of the sanctuary. Beautiful carved wood pillars that appeared twisted flanked the altar as well. Today, the church looks much as it did in the 1800s, as it has been well maintained by residents. Walls that were once adobe and whitewash are now stucco. The hand-painted images of pinto horses have graced the exterior under the balcony since 1915. Four colors—brownish gold, orange, black and white—are widely used on the church itself, while the horses are usually white with turquoise and red embellishments.

One of the most shocking events for early chroniclers of the church's history was the practice of holding native dances inside. This was viewed as a sacrilege at the time, even though the dances were generally held after the residents had attended Mass. Attendees would sit in a circle on the dirt floor, since there were no benches, as the dancers performed in front of the altar and the painted murals of the saints lining the whitewashed interior walls. As with most adobe roofs, it leaked and had to be repaired regularly.

Today, on feast days, the Corn Dance is performed by nearly every member of the pueblo for a number of hours. This carves a ring in the unpaved area in the road in front of the church. This is a rich tradition that dates back hundreds of years. Generally, the pueblo will be open for visitors during these days, but be mindful and courteous of the rules and regulations involved.

Chapter 16

SAN ILDEFONSO

"Where the Water Cuts Through"
Traditional name: P'ohwhoge Owingeh (Po-Wah-Ge Oweenge)
Feast days: January 22–23

A small pueblo consisting of only 750 souls, San Ildefonso Pueblo sits about twenty miles northwest of Santa Fe on over sixty thousand acres of beautiful New Mexico countryside. Dating back to 1300 CE, Pueblo de San Ildefonso was first populated by people from the Mesa Verde region of southern Colorado and then the people of Bandelier as they moved south during the droughts.

As with other pueblos, San Ildefonso is known for its artistry, especially in pottery and jewelry making. The traditional black pottery of the pueblo is highly polished, embellished with matte black designs, which is striking to see. Residents also produce red and polychrome pottery, which is highly desirable.

Maria Montoya Martinez

Noted pueblo potter Maria Martinez, along with her husband, Julian, developed the black-on-black technique that became the identifier for San Ildefonso Pueblo. Born in 1887, Maria Montoya and her four sisters were

Okuwa-Tsire ("Cloud Bird") of San Ildefonso Pueblo, as photographed by Edward S. Curtis in 1905. *Library of Congress.*

taught the art of clay work by their aunt Tia Nicolasa at an early age by making plates to be used in their playhouse. The traditional pottery-making methods had been lost over the years, so Maria and her family studied and developed new techniques to continue their legacy.

It was thought that the black pottery trend started with the Santa Clara Pueblo, since it had produced the highly burnished black pottery since the 1600s. In 1908, archaeologist Edgar Lee Hewett uncovered shards of black-on-white pottery known as biscuit ware that is typically exclusive to the Santa Fe region. Hewett wanted to re-create the pottery style. By doing so, he found Maria Martinez, who was known for her technique of making a great number of thin-walled pots in a short amount of time. He asked her to produce a modern version of the biscuit ware.

During her time making the biscuit ware, Maria experimented with the black-on-black technique she had learned from observing the Tafoya family of Santa Clara Pueblo. The idea behind Maria's methods was to paint red slip on an unfired polished red pot, which is then fired at a cool temperature, producing the glossy background with matte decoration. Other experiments using animal manure and broken pottery shards surrounding the inside and outside of a *hornos* (small outdoor adobe oven) gave the vessels a slicker matte finish.

The quality of the black ware Maria first created was not up to her standards, so she was known to hide these pieces. As the potter's skills advanced, so did the demand for her work. Maria and Julian developed six different processes to complete one pot. After the forming, slipping, burnishing and firing stages were complete, decoration is the icing on the beautiful vessel. Julian discovered that after the *guaco* juice (plants like cactus or spinach, which are boiled long enough to create a thick dark cake) is burned out of the pot by the heat, he could mix the guaco with clay to apply to the burnished pottery with yucca leaves that have been chewed down to a point intricate designs such as roadrunner tracks, feathers, mountains, clouds or zigzags.

The skills of Maria Martinez became so well known, she was invited to the White House on four different occasions, museums worldwide clamored to own a piece of her work and she received honorary doctorates from New Mexico State University and the University of Colorado. Maria's family worked with her to become one of the best-known forces in the Native Arts world. Since Maria's death in 1980, her pottery pieces have escalated in value, with some fetching in the tens of thousands of dollars apiece. This magnificent pottery has been, and continues to be, a great source of income for San Ildefonso Pueblo.

San Ildefonso Mission Church

San Ildefonso Mission Church's history has many twists and turns. During the Entrada, Don Juan de Oñate ordered mission churches built at all the pueblos he encountered, San Ildefonso included. As with its neighbors, the request was more of a forced demand, which led to discord between the Puebloan people and the Spaniards. This treatment lasted for seven decades.

The first permanent church was constructed around 1610 and placed on the northwest side of the pueblo. This structure was eventually destroyed by fire, after the priests were poisoned by the flock during the Pueblo Revolt of 1680. Francisco, San Ildefonso's chief, was one of the foremost leaders of the rebellion and encouraged his people to revolt against Spanish rule.

During the Reconquista of 1692, a second church was said to have been either repaired or rebuilt on the site of the original building. This structure was burned during the Rebellion of 1696, along with two priests, Fray Francisco Corvera and a visiting priest from Nambé Pueblo, Fray Antonio

A "Stairway to the Heavens" at San Ildefonso Pueblo. *Library of Congress.*

Moreno. Their bodies were found four days later by Diego de Vargas, who wrote in his report, "I had the Pecos Indians, and the soldiers cover them with a wall and adobes the rebels had torn down from the church itself for the reason that they could not be moved because they were whole. The fire had not burned them, but rather the smoke and heat suffocated them because the enemy Indians had cut off the ventilation."

By 1706, the third version of the San Ildefonso Mission Church was under construction about one mile north of the present church and was dedicated in 1711. This version was torn down in 1904 by a faction of people not in favor of the "dirt, unsafe old church" when the opposition left the pueblo to attend the St. Louis World's Fair. A new structure was built, described as a schoolhouse with a pitched tin roof, looking nothing like the original mission church. This "practical and tidy church" came down in 1957 and was replaced by a replica of the 1711 mission church. Funds for this construction were raised with bake sales and bazaars. Dedication of this final church was held on December 15, 1968.

Chapter 17

SANTA ANA

Traditional name: Tamayame
Feast day: July 26

No matter how much things change, things stay the same. This holds true on NM 44, on which Santa Ana Pueblo is located. In the late 1600s, travel was perilous, with raiding parties always on the prowl. Today, erratic traffic poses the hazard. Originally, Santa Ana Pueblo was set in a picturesque spot 5,400 feet above sea level against the rocky banks and canyon walls along the Rio Jemez and Rio Grande, which provided isolation and protection. As one of the seven Keres-speaking pueblos in the state, the people of Santa Ana were thought to have migrated out of the Mesa Verde region of present-day Colorado in the 1200s.

Originally known as Tamayame, Santa Ana Pueblo's oral history states that its ancestors rose out of the underworld place known as Shipapa and traveled south. When they reached Kashe Katrukya (Mesa Verde), they stayed only long enough to regain their strength from their long journey. It was at Mesa Verde where the foundations of their life in the "upper world" were established. Pit houses were first built to house the people of the village, which grew to eventually become the pueblo.

After leaving Mesa Verde, the Tamayamians moved even farther south, to Chaco Canyon, where they developed a large community between the twelfth and fourteenth centuries AD. The structures were made from local sandstone and included subterranean places of worship called *kivas*.

The community moved once again, to the Paak'u Village of the Sandia Mountains near Albuquerque.

When Spanish explorers arrived in 1598, an envoy met with Tamayame tribal leaders, who agreed to give allegiance to the Spanish Crown and were given a patron saint, Saint Anne. The name *Santa Ana* would be used from that time forward.

As tensions mounted, Santa Ana Pueblo participated in the Pueblo Revolt of 1680, which drove all the Spaniards from the region in 1680. The people were forced by the Spanish to retreat to nearby Black Mesa and the Jemez Mountains. In 1693, Diego de Vargas returned to the region and coaxed the Pueblo people to return to their village, still used today, twenty-seven miles northwest of Albuquerque. As the people settled back in their village, they began to acquire the land necessary to begin growing crops to supplement the game brought in by hunters.

SANTA ANA PUEBLO MISSION CHURCH

Between 1693 and 1696, Father Custos Francisco de Vargas built a convento while amassing materials such as adobe bricks and log beams to begin the church. Carpenters and laborers were brought over from the Pecos Pueblo to construct the Santa Ana Pueblo Mission Church. Father Dominguez observed that even though the population of the pueblo at this time was upward of three hundred residents, the church was small, measuring four varas wide and seventeen varas long. (The term *vara*—"rod" or "pole" in Spanish—is a unit of measurement used in Latin America equal to thirty-three inches.) Even at this size, the church included a sacristy, ante-sacristy, baptismal and a little walled cemetery. It seemed to the priest that the church was built as a temporary structure.

By 1717, a new convento was standing, featuring a kitchen carved out of the old convento's eight cells, a storeroom and a cloister with two hand-carved wooden doors. In 1734, the new church was being built two varas (almost two yards) above the old foundation and incorporated eighty-four hand-hewn royal pine corbels for the roof, thirty-two medium-sized vigas (wood beams) and three *morillos* (supports), which were brought down from the surrounding mountains by the Pecos Pueblo inhabitants. Eighteen of the vigas were "borrowed" by Alcalde mayor Jose Gonzalez Bas for a chapel he was building at Alameda. This stopped progress on the church at Santa

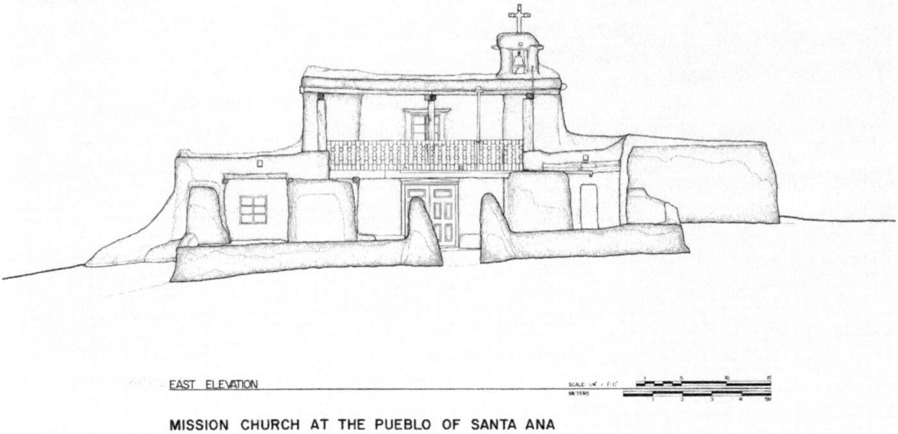

Line drawing of Kewa Pueblo. *Library of Congress.*

Ana for sixteen years. The partial walls of the church stood without any maintenance during this time, until a young priest by the name of Fray Juan Sanz de Lezaun was assigned to the pueblo in 1750 and resumed construction.

Lezaun rallied the pueblo residents by sending the men to the mountains to cut new lumber for the vigas and others to stockpile adobe blocks while he worked alongside them. Due to the pace of the work, the church at Santa Ana was finished in two and a half months. Facing east like the pueblo, the façade of the church and location of the convento were unique, as most faced north. The church was described as having a *mirador* to the south, above the baptistery, with a covered passage from the convento to the sacristy on the north. Santa Ana Pueblo Mission Church also featured a unique six-bay façade, three at ground level and three above the balcony.

A wood altar screen, created by a Laguna Pueblo *santero*, graced the wall behind the small altar. It is said that he was also responsible for the screen at San Felipe Pueblo. A large oil painting of patron saint Saint Anne hung in the sacristy and was lit by the clerestory overhead. The side panels, created by a santero of Santa Ana, did not fare well over time. Two tower belfries framed the arched bell gable over the large wood main doors. Dimensions given in 1881 were fifty-seven feet wide and thirty-five feet high to the foot of the belfries. Father Dominguez writes that, since there was no bell, "necessary summonses were sounded by a war drum."

Unfortunately, even though the population of the pueblo steadily rose, an outbreak of smallpox in 1789–91, as well as other epidemics, threatened to decimate the community. Floods were also a threat, as the pueblo was located on the banks of the Rio Jemez. This made farming difficult and irrigation impossible. As the people began to purchase land on the Rio Grande, they developed Ranchos de Santa Ana, which they initially used seasonally but slowly migrated the entire pueblo to this location. In agreement with Archbishop Peter Bourgade in 1903, the pueblo contracted to maintain a building at the Ranchitos to use as a church while continuing to use and maintain the main chapel, so that they would not be obligated to have a priest celebrate Mass at both chapels.

A leak in the roof developed in 1916, so the pueblo decided to reroof the structure. Vigas were cut from the forest of the Jemez Mountains to be used with raw lumber slabs for the ceiling. A foot of dirt was added to the slabs, but by the 1920s, the roof needed repair again. The Committee for the Preservation and Restoration of the New Mexican Mission Churches offered to pay for a new roof in 1927. The proposal was accepted. The cost of the project was $1,399.62, a huge chunk of change at the time. Unfortunately, the towers were a casualty of this reconstruction.

Present-Day Santa Ana Pueblo

The seventy-nine thousand acres of the present-day pueblo bordered by the town of Bernalillo to the south and Interstate 25 to the east are now supported by gaming operations, including a large casino/hotel that books big-name events and sells Native American foods, blue corn products/plants and Native American apparel.

Santa Ana Pueblo is proud of its roots and traditions, which it shares with the nearby pueblos of Zia and San Felipe. Native traditions still flourish at the pueblo, as they are closely tied to seasons of the sun as it relates to hunting and growing seasons. The combination of traditions introduced to them by the Spanish are also celebrated in the recognition of Catholic feast days. Mass and feasts are merged with the famous pueblo Corn Dance. It is because of this collective thinking that the future of the Santa Ana Pueblo looks bright.

CHAPTER 18

KEWA

Former name: Santo Domingo
Pronunciation: Khe-wa
Feast day: August 4

The people of Kewa Pueblo were first known to live in one of two villages named Gipuy, several miles away from the present-day site. Constant flooding forced the Kewa Pueblo residents to move to the present location, where they were able to concentrate on the development of the community. Kewa is a matrilineal kinship system, which means the children are born into the mother's family and clan, instead of the father's. All inheritance and property pass through the maternal line.

With the arrival of the Spanish in 1598, the Kewa people quickly aligned themselves with the new explorers to garner protection from attacking Apache and Comanche tribes. As a result of this gesture, the Spanish awarded Kewa the name *Santo Domingo* (Saint Dominic) and designated the pueblo a provincial capital and headquarters for the mission system.

MISSION SANTO DOMINGO (KEWA)

When New Spain was divided into missionary districts, the first church at Santo Domingo was built in 1607. It was considered to be an important

Franciscan mission center during the Spanish colonial era. Prone to flooding, the pueblo and the mission church were forced to move at least three times (1780, 1823 and 1830), each time affecting the church.

This alliance between the Spanish and Kewa soon became strained as the raids continued and the Spanish proved themselves to be extremely oppressive. Therefore, Santo Domingo became the staging area for the Pueblo Revolt, when three priests were martyred and the church was burned. Even after the revolt ended and the Spanish tentatively returned in 1692, the relationship between Kewa and the Spanish continued to be volatile.

According to historical documents, a new church was built in approximately 1715 by Fray Antonio Zamora at his own expense. The pueblo now had two churches, standing side by side and facing south. Because of the poor condition, the oldest church was primarily used for burials. Once again, in 1885, a massive flood swept through the pueblo. Even though levees had been installed by the residents, they were forced to remove the doors of the church in order to save the paintings, statues and other precious items from being damaged or swept away.

The flood of June 1886 swept down the Rio Grande Valley, destroying the church and cemetery and leaving a large mound of dirt in their place. Because of this, Kewa Pueblo was without a church for ten years. A new structure was built to replicate the old adobe-style mission.

Said to have one of the best views of the Sandia Mountains in New Mexico, Kewa (formerly Santo Domingo Pueblo) is on the east bank of the Rio Grande, approximately forty miles north of Albuquerque. Even though the pueblo has reverted to its original name, Kewa, the Feast Day of St. Dominic is heavily attended, with upward of one thousand residents to witness the Corn Dance (much like the crowds that gather at San Felipe Pueblo). Members of the squash and turquoise clans perform the Corn Dance, which begins at 10:00 a.m. and goes through the late afternoon, alternating their performances.

The August 4 ceremony draws crowds from across New Mexico and, sometimes, the world. The annual Arts & Crafts Market is also held on feast day. Residents display and sell their beautiful handcrafted jewelry, pottery and traditional food items. A morning Mass and procession is held in the mission church, located at the eastern edge of the Kewa Pueblo. The statue of St. Dominic is carried from the church to the plaza and given a place of honor, remaining there until the dance ceremony is complete.

Kewa Pueblo Mission Church

The brilliant white Kewa Pueblo Mission Church is accented with turquoise and orange paint on the balcony and on gateways to the cemetery in front. Like many other mission churches today, the graveyard is completely covered in soil and the grave sites are not marked. The church is one of the largest and finest living churches in New Mexico.

When the railroad came to New Mexico in 1880–81, it was built along the main thoroughfare, paralleling the El Camino Real, which is now part of Interstate 25. A trading post was built to entice tourists to stop on their travels down Route 66. Its sign claimed, "The Most Interesting Spot in the Old West" and "Where Real Indians Trade." Roadside stands

Santo Domingo Pueblo is now called Kewa Pueblo. *Library of Congress.*

selling pottery, crafts and turquoise jewelry were popular outlets for pueblo artisans. The trading post has been listed in the National Register of Historic Places since 1998.

Jewelry crafted by Kewa Pueblo artisans is unique in that it features beads and native symbols (most widely used is the thunderbird) made from oyster shells, red coral and turquoise inlaid on a serpentine background. Silversmiths also produce stunning works to sell during this celebration. The public is welcome on feast days, but no photography, sketching or videotaping is allowed. As always, follow the rules of the pueblo to have the experience.

PRESENT-DAY KEWA (FORMERLY SANTO DOMINGO PUEBLO)

To find Kewa Pueblo, travel on Interstate 25 between Albuquerque and Santa Fe and take the Santo Domingo exit 259 (the sign has not been changed) from Santa Fe and follow along Highway 22 to Indian Service Road 88. This will take you to the restored Santo Domingo Trading Post. Kewa Pueblo can be reached by turning left, or west. There is also a small museum and gas station at this exit for your enjoyment and convenience. A federally recognized tribe of close to five thousand members, the Kewa People were one of the few Native American tribes who were never displaced from their homelands.

Chapter 19

OHKAY OWINGEH

Yuque Yunque (Place of the Mockingbird)
Former name: San Juan Pueblo (O'ke in Tewa) ("Place of the Strong People")
Feast day: June 24

In March 1598, Spanish conquistador Don Juan de Oñate arrived at Yuque Yunque Pueblo and found the inhabitants to be hospitable and accommodating. The use of the pueblo was offered to the Spaniards, who, in a royal gesture, baptized the community and renamed the neighboring community of Caypa Pueblo, which is present-day Ohkay Owingeh, first San Gabriel and then San Juan de los Caballeros in honor of St. John the Baptist. This established the first Spanish-Catholic capital of New Mexico.

San Juan was Oñate's personal patron saint, and the genteel nature of the natives earned them the status of *caballeros*, or knights. This gesture reunited the segmented communities of the Caypa and Yuque Yunque Pueblos that had drifted apart over the years since these pueblo people arrived at the location.

First visited by Coronado in 1541, the pueblo was not unaccustomed to Spaniards. When Oñate's expedition of over five hundred people and animals encountered the people of Yuque Yunque, they needed shelter and provisions after their three-month journey from Zacatecas, Mexico, in July 1598. Seeing this need, the pueblo kindly offered to move out of Yuque Yunque, one of their five pueblos, and let the Spaniards live there. The offer was accepted, thus establishing the first and oldest Catholic parish in the United States.

A street scene of San Juan Pueblo, now known as Ohkay Owingeh Pueblo. *Library of Congress.*

MANY CHURCHES

The construction of the first of four churches was started on August 23, 1598. Completed in just fifteen days, the structure was large enough to house all the people of the pueblo, although it was crudely constructed from unfinished wood and mud plaster. Historians have said it was made from already formed adobe bricks of ancient homes in the area.

Dedicated to San Miguel (Saint Michael, the archangel), the church celebrated its first Mass on September 8, 1598, when it was also blessed and consecrated by the priests who had accompanied Oñate. A weeklong celebration followed that included a bullfight, a play written especially for the occasion, battle reenactments and a tilting tournament. A second, more structurally sound church, also in San Gabriel, was built on the same foundation a few years later. The second foundation, measuring seventy feet long, sixty feet wide in the transepts and thirty feet wide in the main lobby was unearthed in 1959.

San Juan Bautista Church

The Spanish mission system was formally set up after the Reconquista of 1692, when a new church was built on the foundation of the structure that had been destroyed in 1680. It was in Ohkay Owingeh that an important figure in pueblo history was born. Popé, or Po'pay, a religious leader from the pueblo, would go on to organize the largest indigenous rebellion in New Mexico, the Pueblo Revolt of 1680. A statue in Popé's honor was erected at the pueblo in 2005, when the pueblo reverted to its traditional name.

San Juan Bautista (St. John the Baptist) Mission Church was destroyed during the Pueblo Revolt. Construction on a new church would not begin until the Spanish returned in 1692. This church would last an astounding fifty years before a new one was necessary in 1760.

Measuring 22 feet wide and 110 feet long, the new church had a single bell tower, and the hand-painted altar screen was colorfully decorated in yellows, blues and reds. A combination of cultures existed in harmony in San Juan Bautista Mission Church, as the interior was decorated with murals of the saints as well as buffalo hides until 1826, when it became secularized.

Reroofing of the adobe church occurred in the mid-nineteenth century, and the church was maintained until the arrival of Padre Camilo from France in 1865. He had a disdain for adobe structures and knocked down the old church. In its place, on the same footprint, was constructed a two-story rectory, a school and a neo-Gothic church in brick. Today, San Juan Bautista Mission Church continues to be an active Catholic parish where hymns are sung in Tewa and Spanish.

Present-Day Ohkay Owingeh (formerly San Juan Pueblo)

Today, Ohkay Owingeh is the headquarters for the Eight Northern Pueblos Council and is one of the largest Tewa-speaking pueblos in New Mexico. As with other pueblos, Ohkay Owingeh is involved in the gaming industry and owns the Ohkay Casino along Interstate 25. A long history of redware pottery making, weaving and painting by members of Ohkay Owingeh and neighboring pueblos is on display at the pueblo-owned Oke-Oweenge Crafts Cooperative. There is a fee for photos, sketching and videos.

San Juan lies twenty-five miles north of Santa Fe on US 84/285 and five miles north of Española off NM 68.

Chapter 20

TAOS

"Place of Red Willows"
Traditional name: Tuah-Tah
Feast days: June 13, June 24, July 25–26, September 30

On the slight outskirts of Taos, New Mexico, sits a beautiful, multistoried pueblo that has been occupied for one thousand years and is considered one of the oldest continuously inhabited communities in the United States. Due to this distinction, the Taos Pueblo is now a UNESCO World Heritage Site and National Historic Landmark.

The haphazard stepped pyramid-style structure rises out of the high desert clay against the majestic backdrop of the Sangre de Cristo (Blood of Christ) Mountains. No, it is not your imagination that the buckskin-hued adobe accented by wood-framed windows painted turquoise have a sparkle. This glint, caused by the high mica mineral content of the soil from which the adobe bricks and mud covering were made, let fuel to the perpetuation of rumors that Taos Pueblo was a "Golden City." As the Spaniards realized the stories were false, their mood darkened accordingly. The natives used the desires of the conquistadors against them by creating stories of cities with great wealth; unfortunately these backfired, as the explorers did not appreciate being duped when the truth came out.

Often touted as a magical event, the Christmas Eve Procession of the Virgin Mary in the Taos Pueblo Plaza is a large draw to the ancient settlement. Bonfires of ocote (pine) wood line the route of the procession attendees as

Inhabited for over one thousand years, Taos Pueblo was thought to have been one of the "Seven Cities of Gold." *Library of Congress.*

they carry a statue of the Blessed Mother to the Plaza while singing religious hymns. La Nocha Buena (the good night) and La Navidad (Christmas, the birth of Christ) are celebrated with a statue of Mary being carried from the San Geronimo Chapel to the Plaza followed by dancers, drummers and women singing in the native tongue of Tewa along with English.

San Geronimo Chapel

Construction of the first mission church at Taos Pueblo was difficult due to the reported "non-cooperation" of the residents. Fray Miranda and several Spaniards were killed, and the church was destroyed in 1640 by the Taos people, causing them to leave the Pueblo. Charges of immorality of the assigned priest was sent to the Spanish Inquisition in Mexico in 1647 by the tribe, so it took until 1660 for the pueblo to accept another priest. As the new church began to be built, relations deteriorated as the practice of the collection of tribute continued and the pueblo's traditional religious rites were extinguished.

Taos Mission Church was built after the original was partially destroyed. *Library of Congress.*

The Pueblo Revolt of 1680 destroyed the new church and was left in ruins until the Reconquista in 1692, when it was discovered to have been used as a stable in the interim. Diego de Vargas ordered the church destroyed since it was irreparable. Franciscan friars did not return to the region until 1706, when they rebuilt the church once again. This version of the church was finished in 1726 and stood until 1846.

Made of adobe with square bell towers, the third church was on the outskirts of the pueblo compounds and faced another uprising, which would be the end of this structure. In 1846, the natives and Mexicans opposed the American takeover of New Mexico during the Mexican American War.

The natives took refuge in San Geronimo Chapel thinking the three- to seven-foot-thick walls would give protection. The American troops lobbed cannonballs at the dissidents, but to no avail—the artillery became lodged in the adobe walls. Seeing this strategy did not work, the church's roof was set on fire, allowing the troops to storm the building. This church was left as a reminder to ruin as a new church was built in 1850. This is the structure you see today as you tour the Taos Pueblo, and the former church now serves as a cemetery for the many generations of native and Spanish peoples.

Chapter 21

SANDIA

Traditional name: Tuf Shur Tia ("Green Reed Place")
Pronunciation: San-DEE-ah

The Sandia Pueblo, located along the banks of the Rio Grande, was traditionally called Tuf Shur Tia ("green reed place") because of the foliage along the river. But if you have ever witnessed a sunset in Albuquerque, New Mexico, you will have no doubt why the range to the east of the city is called the Sandia Mountains. *Sandia* ("watermelon" in Spanish) is a perfect name for the rugged mountains that slowly turn from purple to a gorgeous shade of reddish pink in the late-day sun.

Comprising seven hundred acres of land, Sandia is one of the smallest pueblos in terms of acreage in northern New Mexico. It is located just three miles south of Bernalillo off Highway 85. Sandia Pueblo has had several names over the years: Nafiat ("at the dusty place"), Tuf Shur Tia, San Francisco de Sandia, Nuestra Señora de los Delores de Sandia, Nuestra Señora del los Delores y San Antonio de Sandia and, finally, Sandia Pueblo, or Pueblo of Sandia.

Developed between AD 700 and 1100, Sandia had a population of around three thousand souls by the time Francisco Vázquez de Coronado arrived in 1539. He claimed to have discovered the settlement. The years 1100 to 1300 are referred to as the Great Pueblo Period, a time of cooperation between all of the Pueblo people and of the Great Kiva ritual, which was a group effort.

NUESTRA SEÑORA DE LOS DELORES

Fray Esteban de Perea, an authority for the Spanish Inquisition, arrived in 1610 and established Nuestra Señora de los Delores (Our Lady of Sorrows) at Sandia Pueblo. The priest had many conflicts with the various Spanish governors of the region until he left Sandia in 1621. One such conflict was the arrest and detention of Governor Pedro de Peralta in 1613 by Fray Isidro Ordóñez, who chained and imprisoned the official in the mission at Sandia Pueblo. Perea did not agree with the actions but was obedient and complied. Even though Perea became the head of the Catholic Church in New Mexico in 1617, he continued to have disputes with the governors as well as with the viceroy of New Spain, who regulated him due to the complaints of abuse from the Sandia Pueblo people.

Perea left his office in 1621 but remained in New Mexico temporarily. Consideration was being taken by Spain and the Franciscan order to abandon New Mexico altogether because of the strife between the church and the state, but at Perea's urging, the mission continued. In fact, thirty more missionaries were sent in 1629, when the priest returned to New Mexico as well. It is reported that by the end of 1629 there were upward of forty-six priests working to convert the population to Catholicism. The mistreatment, taxes on crops and cotton and forced labor of the Sandia Pueblo residents, as with the other pueblos, caused deep resentment toward the Spanish.

PART II

NON-PUEBLO MISSIONS

Chapter 22

SIGNIFICANT NON-PUEBLO CHURCHES

San Miguel Chapel, Santa Fe

Located in the oldest capital city of the United States, Santa Fe, San Miguel Chapel is known as the oldest church in the United States by historians and is referred to as the "Oldest Church" by Santa Fe residents. The actual date of construction is still debated, but rare records mentioning the adobe chapel date it to at least 1628. It is now a United States National Landmark.

Most believe that San Miguel Chapel was built in 1610 by the Tlaxcala ("Tas-cal-en") Indians, who originated in Mexico and followed Spanish explorer Don Juan Oñate y Salazar and Franciscan friars. The Tlaxcala erected the sacred building in what is now known as the Barrio de Anaico Historical District over an ancient kiva of the Analco Indians on the south side of the Santa Fe River. This act is thought to be significant, as the Spaniards disallowed the local indigenous people from practicing their religious traditions. By having the chapel built over the kiva, they retained a small connection to their religion.

Built to serve the laborers, soldiers and Indians who lived in the barrio, San Miguel Chapel was first christened Hermita de San Miguel. Franciscan friars who made the Entrada of 1598 with Don Juan Oñate enlisted the labor of the locals to build the adobe structure, which was destined to see many transformations.

San Miguel Chapel has witnessed much turmoil in New Mexico's past.

Provincial Governor Luis de Rojas (Rosas)

The Spaniards, notorious for their cruelty to the residents, were led by Ninth Provincial Governor Luis de Rojas (sometimes written Rosas) from 1637 to 1641. During this time, the Puebloan people were enslaved by Rojas, who forced them to weave items for his shop, work in his home and fields and build churches.

Rojas made many enemies in the church community, which experienced the official's cruelty firsthand. Hoping to come to a compromise, two Franciscan friars went to Santa Fe to meet with Rojas, who beat them both bloody with a stick in the middle of the road in front of San Miguel Chapel. The friars had clashed with the governor many times over his extremely poor treatment of the locals, and the Catholic Church was threatening to excommunicate him if his actions did not cease. Rojas's message was made clear through his abhorrent actions.

San Miguel Chapel Interior

If the large, waxed wood beams on the ceiling of San Miguel Chapel could recount the amazing history that occurred within its whitewashed adobe walls, we would quite possibly know more than what has already been revealed. Those who sat on the oak and pine pews in front of the wooden communion rail could marvel at the beauty of the wood hand-painted three-stage *retablos* (frescos) framed in vivid green on the back wall behind the altar, which houses a hand-carved wood statue of St. Michael (San Miguel), brought from Mexico in 1709 by Franciscan friars and placed in the chapel in 1798. Each feature is illuminated by side windows that let in the warm New Mexico light. Carved wood relief Stations of the Cross and crucifixes line each side of the chapel interior. They recall the Passion of Christ. The interior setting is intimate and still sees Mass performed each Sunday. San Miguel Chapel is also the site of one of the oldest cemeteries in the Southwest, barely edged out by Acoma Pueblo, which contains records of burials dating to 1629.

Interior of the oldest church in the United States. *Library of Congress.*

LORETTO CHAPEL, SANTA FE

Nestled deep in the heart of the City of Holy Faith, otherwise known as Santa Fe, the spires of Loretto Chapel rise up in gray French Gothic splendor among the adobe, flat-roofed structures that surround the church. Modeled after Archbishop Jean-Baptiste Lamy's favorite Sainte Chapelle, or "Holy Chapel," which is in the courtyard of the royal palace in Paris, Loretto Chapel's construction began in 1873.

Once construction was complete, the architect died, and it was found that he had left no access to the choir loft, which was twenty feet above the

The Gothic architecture of Loretto Chapel reminds one of Notre Dame Cathedral.

body of the chapel. A normal staircase would have impeded the number of worshipers, since it would have taken up valuable real estate in the church. The sisters of Loretto Chapel were perplexed as to what to do to safely access their beautiful choir loft.

The legend of this stunningly beautiful chapel states that the seven sisters prayed a nine-day petition novena (a special prayer) to Saint Joseph, the patron saint of carpenters, passionately believing their prayers would be answered. Folklore states that on the ninth day, once the novena was complete, a stranger seeking refuge appeared at the chapel door with a donkey loaded with tools. The stranger had no money to pay for board, but he was willing to trade his labor as a carpenter for his room and board. The sisters of Loretto Chapel rejoiced and quickly accepted the man's offer, knowing that their prayers had been truly answered.

A gorgeous spiral staircase constructed without the use of nails was the result of the stranger's efforts. Now the sisters of Loretto Chapel had access to their choir loft. For the safety of the nuns, railing was added later because of the steep ascent. Today, this staircase is a huge tourist attraction for the chapel and considered a miracle for the way it was constructed.

Right: Home to the Miraculous Staircase, Loretto Chapel is a stunning Gothic beauty surrounded by adobe.

Opposite: Thought to have been built by Saint Joseph, the Miraculous Staircase was constructed without nails.

CATHEDRAL BASILICA OF ST. FRANCIS OF ASSISI, SANTA FE

Built with the instruction of Archbishop Jean-Baptiste Lamy, who favored the French Gothic architecture of his homeland, the Cathedral Basilica is a sharp contrast to the surrounding adobe structures of Santa Fe, or, as it is known, the "City Different." In the heart of the capital city, the Cathedral Basilica of St. Francis of Assisi has been standing tall and proud since 1850.

Situated on the footprint of the two original adobe churches at this site—one built in 1626 but destroyed in the Pueblo Revolt of 1680, and the other, La Parroquia, also an adobe church built between 1714 and 1717—the new cathedral, completed in 1887, was built in the Romanesque style by French architects and Italian stonemasons. Archbishop Lamy had a disdain for adobe architecture and insisted any church he commissioned be of Gothic European design without the use of any offending "mud."

St. Francis Cathedral was built directly over the complete structure of the La Parroquia chapel, which was then dismantled and brought out of

Archbishop Jean-Baptiste Lamy built St. Francis Cathedral in his favorite Romanesque style.

St. Francis Catheral was originally designed with tall spires, but due to budget constraints, only the platforms were built. *Library of Congress.*

the enormous brass front doors of the new cathedral piece by piece. The French-made stained-glass windows around the lower bay of the structure feature the twelve apostles, and a magnificent round stained-glass rose window installed over the front paneled bronze door is reminiscent of the Rose Window in Notre Dame Cathedral. Seven archbishops, including Lamy, are buried in the sanctuary.

The cathedral was elevated to the status of a basilica by Pope Benedict XVI in 2005. This denotes a church of great importance to Rome as well as one with a history of spreading Catholicism in the world.

OUR LADY OF GUADALUPE SHRINE, SANTA FE

Built in 1776, the year of the United States' declaration of independence from England, Our Lady of Guadalupe Church in the capital city of Santa Fe is known as the oldest still-standing shrine honoring Our Lady of Guadalupe in America. In the heart of the historic Guadalupe District between the now revitalized railyard and the center of the "City Different," Our Lady of Guadalupe Church is home to over one thousand families.

Devotion to Our Lady of Guadalupe in the New World grew in the seventeenth and eighteenth centuries as the symbol was brought north along the Rio Grande by Spanish colonists. Today, the image of Our Lady of Guadalupe is recognized worldwide. She is known as the "Patroness of the Americas." On her feast day, December 12, processions, dances and private devotions are performed in her honor.

Our Lady of Guadalupe Legend

Completed in 1795, the adobe church was dedicated to Our Lady of Guadalupe, an icon of Hispanic culture. Mary, the mother of Jesus, appeared to Juan Diego in 1531. Diego, a recent convert and now the first Catholic indigenous saint from the Americas, canonized in 2002, was born in Cuautitlán, Mexico, in 1474.

During one of his many walks to the Franciscan mission where he was receiving religious instruction, Diego was granted his first of five visitations from the Virgin Mary on a hill at Tepeyac, Mexico, on December 9, 1531. In this visitation, Mother Mary asked Diego to request that the bishop build a church in her honor so the faithful would have a place to go and pray. Diego immediately granted her request, but the bishop was skeptical. Later that day, Mary appeared to Diego a second time, during which Diego sadly told her of his failure to convey her instructions. He stated that he was a man of no means and of no importance and that it would be best if she found someone else for her task. After this visitation, Diego returned to the bishop a second time to relay his mission. The bishop was less skeptical this time but asked for a sign to prove that the apparition to which Diego was referring was from heaven.

Returning to Tepeyac a third time, the Virgin Mary heard the bishop's request and said she would return the next day to provide proof. Diego's uncle became deathly ill overnight, so Diego went to find a priest to take his uncle's confession instead of meeting with the Virgin Mary the next day as promised, which embarrassed him terribly. Mary asked him why he had not come to her, for she was his mother. She also related that his uncle was recovered, so Diego was to climb the hill and gather the flowers he would find growing there. What Diego found astounded him. The hill was

The image of Our Lady of Guadalupe is one of the most popular religious icons in the Southwest and Mexico.

Our Lady of Guadalupe Shrine sits in the heart of Santa Fe.

covered with hundreds of flowers unseasonably blooming in the winter where before only cactus grew.

Diego gathered the flowers in his cape and returned to the Virgin Mary, who rearranged the flowers and told him to take them to the bishop. Obliging, Diego returned to the bishop, and as he opened his mantle in front of the priest, not only did a multitude of different flowers—such as Castilian roses, lilies, carnations, violets, jasmine and rosemary—not native to Mexico spill out at his feet, but an image of the Virgin was also imprinted on the inside of the cloak. The bishop was then convinced by Diego's story. Juan Diego's mantle was kept in the bishop's private chapel at first and then displayed in the church. This mantle and Saint Juan Diego have been connected to many reports of miracles over the centuries, even as recent as 1990.

When Diego returned home, he indeed found that his uncle was well and had a story of his own to tell. He related that he had been visited by a beautiful woman whom he knew to be the Virgin Mary, who told him to tell the bishop of his miraculous recovery, the visitation and her wish to be known under the title of Guadalupe. Images of Our Lady of Guadalupe are striking and usually show Our Lady surrounded by red Castilian roses. Her beautiful image has become the most popular cultural symbol of Mexico and can be found throughout the Southwest as well. Many studies of the mantle have been conducted to discredit the validity of the garment, yet none have been able to completely disprove the miracle.

SAN FELIPE DE NERI, ALBUQUERQUE

Standing proudly at the north end of the Old Town Plaza in Albuquerque, New Mexico, San Felipe de Neri grounds the community square; the parishioners like to call themselves the "Spiritual Heart of Albuquerque." This magnificently restored church has seen much history since construction of the original adobe structure began in 1793. The original church collapsed due to flooding and heavy rains that plagued Albuquerque in the 1700s. It is fortuitous that Archbishop Jean-Baptiste Lamy despised adobe and had the next church accessorized with Gothic touches in his favored Romanesque style. Two spires were added to the adobe cruciform church, giving it a European flair.

The interior includes tongue-and-groove wood wainscoting, a stamped tin ceiling, an elegant altar and plaster walls that were painted to resemble

Left: San Felipe de Neri graces the north end of Old Town Plaza in Albuquerque.

Opposite: Damaged by floods, San Felipe de Neri has been beautifully restored.

marble. Most of these features were added around 1916. Marble was an expensive material to use and to transport to the Southwest. Five-foot-thick adobe walls support the ceiling and spires. A high ceiling is supported with wood vigas and carved corbel.

One notable tidbit of history involved the American Civil War. Albuquerque was the site of a short-lived battle and had been captured by the Confederate army. The Union army was able to recapture the village and leased San Felipe de Neri's rectory for several years for its use. The rectory was built with a second story and a widow's walk.

The original church was built closer to the center of Old Town Plaza and included a cemetery. When the huge floods occurred, they unfortunately on occasion exposed graves and bones. The bones were gathered and finally interred in the concrete of the left spire, as they could not be identified. It is an honor to be included in a church structure for burial. Mass is still being said in San Felipe de Neri. There is no fee to visit this beautiful church

surrounded by rose gardens, but please visit the gift shop to make a purchase, as the funds are used for maintenance. San Felipe de Neri Church is one of the oldest buildings in Albuquerque and the only building in Old Town dating to the Spanish colonial period.

OUR LADY OF LIGHT MISSION CHAPEL, LAMY

The town of Lamy was named after famed Archbishop Jean-Baptiste Lamy, who had the Cathedral Basilica of St. Francis of Assisi built in Santa Fe, eighteen miles away. As the closest train stop to the capital city, Lamy was an active town consisting of the historic Legal Tender restaurant, the Annex Saloon, a school and the luxurious El Ortiz Hotel, built by the Fred Harvey Company in 1896. The hills surrounding Santa Fe were too precarious to allow for the construction of railways; the outskirts offered a better, more level prospect. The Atchison, Topeka and Santa Fe (ATSF) Railroad, now the Burlington Northern Santa Fe (BNSF) Railroad, ran this line until 2014.

Our Lady of Light Mission Chapel was constructed in 1926 in the Mission Revival style for the Catholic community and served it well until 1994, when it was deconsecrated due to the population decline in Lamy. This also meant that there were not enough parishioners to warrant a priest. This historically important church, on a site in the middle of the historic Lamy Land Grant where acreage was taken in trust, was deemed structurally unsound by the mid-1990s. This architectural style was exceedingly rare for northern New Mexico, and the state placed the chapel in the State Register of Cultural Properties. The El Ortiz Hotel and the train depot were also created in the Mission Revival style.

The same footprint for a church built around 1889 was used for the modern structure. A flood was said to have destroyed the first church. A stone at the church reads "Nuestra Señora de la Luz, 1900."

Restoration efforts are being made by the Our Lady of Light Historic Foundation to restore the chapel to its former glory. Stained-glass windows still glow in the setting sun, and a representation of a bell is painted on the wood in the belfry for authenticity. Lamy is a quiet, charming hamlet off Highway 28, fourteen and a half miles from the hustle and bustle of Santa Fe. It's recommended you take the short detour if you are in the vicinity to see this historic town for yourself.

Our Lady of Light Mission Church in Lamy.

SAN MIGUEL CHURCH, SOCORRO

With the Entrada of 1598 by Spanish conquistador Don Juan de Oñate y Salazar and his party, the inhabitants of Socorro were generous to the explorers, providing supplies such as corn for his people when they arrived.

San Miguel Church in Socorro once boasted a solid silver communion rail.

Because of this kindness, Oñate left two Franciscan friars behind to establish a mission in the region. It was Fray Alfonso Benavidez who gave the small settlement the name *Nuestra Senora de Perpetus Socorro* (Our Lady of Perpetual Help) as an expression of gratitude to the village. Later, the village, which today has approximately ten thousand residents, was renamed Socorro, which means literally to "give aid."

On a western spoke radiating from the roundabout in the center of the historic district of Socorro, New Mexico, is San Miguel Church. With the help of the native people in the area, a church was built between 1615 and 1626. This church replaced an earlier structure on the same spot. It was well built. Adobe was used to make five-foot-thick walls, and the structure featured massive corbels, beams and vigas, the latter hand-carved from local pine cut and hauled in from the mountains. The windows of the church were placed high to offer protection for those inside from attacking native tribes, in this case, the Navajo, who had no trouble gaining access to lower windows.

Mining was the main industry for the area around Socorro due to the astounding amount of silver ore located in the surrounding mountains. The ore was in such abundance, in fact, that it is written that the communion rail, chalices and tabernacle in San Miguel Church were made of the precious metal. The artistry of the local silversmiths was legendary, so their skills were utilized to create artwork for the interior of the church. The priests noted in their reports that the pieces of art were as fine as anything in Spain or Mexico. When word was received of the Pueblo Revolt in 1680, the priests had all the treasures from the church removed and buried far away to protect them in the case of looting. A map was made of the location so that the artifacts could be recovered later.

Most of the native population who lived in Socorro and outlying areas followed the priests to the El Paso region during the Pueblo Revolt to escape the violence.

ST. FRANCIS DE ASÍS, GOLDEN

Perched on a hill just off NM 14, also known as the Turquoise Trail, is one of the most photographed churches in northern New Mexico. St. Francis de Asís Church, also known as San Francisco Catholic Church, was built in 1830 in. Restored in the 1960s by historian and author Fray Angelico Chavez while he was the priest at St. Joseph's Church in Los Cerrillos, St. Francis is now being lovingly maintained by members of the Montaño family after being abandoned for over twenty-five years. Because of the efforts of Michael Montaño and other parishioners, Mass is still said every Saturday afternoon.

Surrounded by 3,605 mines, Golden has been a popular mining community since the discovery of precious metals in 1825 caused the first gold rush west of the Mississippi. Originally named Real de San Francisco

St. Francis de Asís Church in Golden has been lovingly restored by the Montaño family.

and Placer del Tuerto, the two steadily growing mining communities merged to form one large village that was then named Golden. Gold deposits began to dwindle by 1884, as did the population. By 1928, the gold and the population had diminished so much that the post office closed and Golden was rendered a ghost town.

Spaniards and Native Americans first worked the turquoise, gold, silver and lead mines scattered throughout the Ortiz Mountains until the Anglos began to stop on their way to the gold fields in California. Ruins of these workings can be seen along the Turquoise Trail directly across from St. Francis Church. A word of warning: be sure to keep a sharp eye out for St. Francis Church, as it pops into sight fast when you are traveling and is partially hidden by a hill and trees. Wooden and concrete crosses grace the oldest of the graves in the courtyard.

High Road to Taos

Once you've visited the Santuario de Chimayó, continue on through the quaint village to the *T* in the road, then turn right on SR-76. This will take you on a magical journey through the high-desert landscape from Chimayó to Taos, New Mexico. Along this fifty-six-mile scenic byway route, you will encounter historic hamlets that are sure to take your breath away. Be sure to patronize the many artist galleries and gift shops along the route for one-of-a-kind mementos. Each village has a specialty item for which it is known, such as handwoven blankets, folk wood carvings, sculpture, pottery, paintings and fine photography.

If you veer off the High Road into one of the tiny hamlets, be sure to watch out for wildlife and domesticated animals on the road. Cows, dogs and a pair of alpacas have been encountered wandering the roadways along this route.

Santuario de Chimayó, Chimayó

Tucked off NM 76, the Santuario de Chimayó can also be accessed from NM 503, which exits Highway 84/285 a few miles north of Pojoaque, New Mexico. This route is a narrow yet picturesque, winding two-lane road that

Left: The Vigil Store in Chimayó sells delicious red chile.

Opposite: Santuario de Chimayó hosts thousands of pilgrims each year during Holy Week.

takes you through both residential areas and pueblos. Coyote fencing, adobe homes and cottonwood trees draping over the roadway create the scene for a gorgeous painting worthy of any Santa Fe gallery.

From NM 503 you will turn left and, along NM 520, pass through the wild badlands countryside that includes sandstone formations known as hoodoos as well as eroded, striated mesas in shades of red, white and yellow. Drop down into the Chimayó Valley and you will be greeted by a quaint village that promotes its most famous attraction, the Santuario de Chimayó.

Holy dirt taken from a hole in the Santuario is touted as having healing qualities. Great quantities of discarded crutches are left at the church as a testament to the power of the blessed soil. A golden crucifix was reportedly taken from the spot where the dirt is extracted in the Santuario today and brought to a priest several miles away. The next day, the golden cross was discovered missing from its new home, only to be discovered in the original

location again. This transition occurred three times. The Santuario was built around the cross, which is still displayed on the sacred altar.

Each year during Holy Week, the road to the Santuario is lined with thousands of faithful pilgrims who walk to the church (sometimes on their knees) from as far away as Albuquerque and Santa Fe to attend Mass on Easter Sunday. The small church fills to the brim with believers. Of all the mission churches in New Mexico, I believe, personally, that Santuario de Chimayó has the most spiritual feel and is known as the "most sacred spot in New Mexico."

Surrounding the Santuario are shops selling religious items, tortillas, Chimayó's famous red chile and highly prized hand-woven Chimayó blankets.

NUESTRA SEÑORA DEL ROSARIO, TRUCHAS (1764, 1784, 1805)

Truchas, which traditionally means "trout," can also mean "careful" when used as a command. The present-day village, steeped in history and inspiration, is perched along the rim of a high ridge above a valley of magnificent pine trees that cascades down the mountainside to the lower elevation. This precarious location more than eight thousand feet above the valley floor may be the reason for the "careful" interpretation.

As a setting for Robert Redford's film *The Milagro Beanfield War*, Truchas garnered the attention of artists drawn to this breathtakingly beautiful scenery to create their works of art. An artist could get a serious case of whiplash with such beauty on both sides of the road. Lush green mountain meadows ringed with cottonwood trees and colorful-roofed adobe houses against the bluish-purple Truchas Peaks offer the backdrop for a painting that needs no enhancements.

Just past the left-hand turn as you continue your trek on the High Road to Taos (NM 76) is Nuestra Señora del Rosario (Our Lady of the Rosary) Church. You can barely see it from the road, so it is extremely easy to miss. In addition, there is no grand entrance to the church to guide you there. At the intersection of NM 75 (straight) and NM 76 (left-hand turn), go straight for the length of a building. There will be a road that looks like an alley to the extreme right as you pass the first adobe structure at the intersection. The small one-lane dirt path will open in front of the historic church building in a small parking area.

Nuestra Señora del Rosario in Truchas.

SAN JOSE DE GARCIA CHURCH, LAS TRAMPAS

Santo Tomas Apostol del Rio de Las Trampas, known commonly as Las Trampas or Trampas, is an eighteenth-century village that is part of the National Historical Landmark District (1967) along the High Road to Taos (New Mexico State Road 76) in the Sangre de Cristo Mountains of Taos County. Take the extra time to travel this narrow two-lane enchanted road and be immersed in the history and stunning beauty of the countryside. Gift shops and galleries tucked into the tiny hamlets wait for you to stop. You will be surprised at the treasures you can discover. Trampas is the Spanish word for "traps," and a drive along NM SR 76, especially during the fall, will capture your heart forever.

First settled by twelve Spanish families from Santa Fe in 1751, Las Trampas was the second Genizaro village in the region, the first being Belen, outside of Albuquerque. The term *Genizaro* (which is considered to be derogatory) means "de-tribalized." Native Americans were taken from their homes as captives by other tribes to then be sold as servants or laborers for Spanish and Mexican families in northern New Mexico and southern Colorado. Children of Spanish masters and native slaves are also referred to as "coyotes." It is reported that these slaves were mistreated and considered to be of the lowest of castes in the communities. Spanish, the primary language spoken, is mixed with the Tanoan dialect of the Taos Pueblo as well as their native tongues of Comanche and Apache.

Las Trampas was set up as a defensive community to protect the village of Santa Cruz, which is seventeen miles southwest, against constant attacks by the Utes, Comanche and Apache who roamed the area looking for slaves. A central plaza was ringed with homes, and all were protected by a defensive wall. By 1776, the original twelve families had increased to sixty-three. The community was described on many occasions as "a ragged lot…as festive as they are poor, and very merry."

Since the nearest church was ten miles away at the Picuris Pueblo, San Jose de Gracia Church was built between the years 1760 and 1776 to service Las Trampas. As one of the more original Spanish colonial Pueblo mission churches still existing in New Mexico, San Jose de Garcia was given the distinction of becoming a National Historic Landmark in 1967 and is in the United States Register of Historic Places.

Built in the traditional cruciform style, San Jose de Garcia proudly takes its place on the east side of the dirt plaza. Four- to six-foot-thick plaster walls hold a single nave one hundred feet long and fifty-two feet wide decorated with a main altar screen painted with religious images in 1860 by Jose de Garcia Gonzales, a Mexico *santero*. A distinctive feature of the nave is a clerestory window placed just right to illuminate the apse area; the church is otherwise lit only with candles. This type of window is unheard of in New Mexico, especially related to the Spanish colonial times. The southern entrance of the nave is flanked with buttresses topped with wood belfries. Wide-plank wood floors are found throughout the church, including in the choir loft and balcony, of which this church had two. The roof built between the belfries helped the bell ringer to crawl out of one window and cross over to the other. Previously, this poor soul had to travel back and forth numerous times to ring the bells.

Due to the high cost of transporting corrugated iron roofing, San Jose was spared the new tradition of placing peaked roofs on the mission churches. In 1921, the roof began to leak, and it was determined that it would cost $1,000 to $1,200 to replace. The Museum of New Mexico was called in to advise what to do in this situation. The Museum of New Mexico was able to save the church once again from a "disfiguring iron roof" by suggesting the balcony and belfries could be restored using the original tar and gravel roof, which would last at least twenty years and cost a fraction of the amount originally quoted. Unfortunately, other projects of the Committee for the Preservation and Restoration of the New Mexican Mission Churches took precedence. The roof would not be fixed for ten more years. This restoration left the church without belfries, which would not be restored until 1967.

Funds raised by concerned citizens of Santa Fe were used to replace and restore the roof, bell towers and balcony beams and supplied new windows to be inserted in the adobe walls—all for $1,175.37. Even during the Depression, this was considered a low price. The preservationists who funded the project think of the historic church as a sacred trust.

In 1966, the New Mexico Highway Department was set to widen NM 76, which ran straight through Las Trampas. Initial drawings showed the road cutting across the walled churchyard to pass within feet of the historic church. Once again, preservationists objected loudly on a fight that garnered national attention. After much work and debate, the highway project was delayed, and the historic significance of Las Trampas was addressed. Residents saw it another way, protesting to have the road installed. As a result, the Las Trampas Foundation applied for National Landmark status for the church, which was granted in 1967.

As with many other mission churches of the pueblos, it is the women of the community who apply new plaster to the walls of the buildings each year. In the walled forecourt of the church rest generations of residents of Las Trampas who have gone on to their final reward. Many graves in the northern part of the yard are now unidentifiable, a result of weathered and eroded wood markers. Most of the more recent graves now lie to the south of the church.

Another outstanding feature of the nave is the ceiling, supported by wood vigas that are covered with painted planks that run the entire span of the church. This roof has been replaced several times during the lifetime of the church, including in 1932, when famed architect John Gaw Meem led the Society for the Preservation of New Mexico Mission Churches. The ceiling of the entrance is once again decorated with eighteenth- and nineteenth-century paintings of the saints, mirroring the artwork inside the sanctuary.

Left: San Jose de Garcia Church watches over the village of Las Trampas.

Below: Hand-carved doors grace the entrance of San Jose de Garcia Church.

Interior of San Jose de Garcia Church in Las Trampas.

An inscription over the front doors states they were carved by Nicolas D. Apodaca, who was a local artist.

Unfortunately, the church is locked during the week, but it is open to visitors on the weekend. The original façade needs a bit of repair and paint, but you can walk among the lonely graves and reflect on the setting at your leisure. At the entrance to the walkway to the church, you will ascend steps made from old railroad timbers through a heavy, hand-carved, weathered wood gate that hangs open from a tall adobe frame. San Jose de Garcia Church is accessible and visible from the dirt road slightly off NM 76.

An annual tradition includes the plastering and whitewashing of the adobe walls, inside and out. The interior of the church is said to be highly decorated and includes a hooded wood figure of a woman representing death: Doña Sebastiana or Santa Muerte (Saint of Death). As part of the Penitente Brotherhood, which is a darker, more extreme form of Christianity, Doña Sebastiana has come to represent St. Sebastian, who was shot by many arrows and still survived. The legend morphed together in Mexico, where Doña Sebastiana is said to visit a village every year, when she "shoots" one person she has chosen to give up his life for religion; he is known as a martyr. Doña's image is generally represented by a carved skeleton sitting in a wood cart with a bow and arrow and is a large icon of northern New Mexico and Penitente traditions.

San Francisco de Assisi Church Mission Church, Ranchos de Taos

Thanks to artists such as Georgia O'Keeffe and Ansel Adams, the chapel of St. Francis de Assisi (St. Francis of Assisi) in Rancho de Taos is one of the most recognizable images of Taos and the Southwest. Positioned in the heart of Rancho de Taos, a suburb of the village of Taos, New Mexico, the famous church harkens back to ancient times. Built over two hundred years ago, between 1772 and 1816, San Francisco de Assisi is the only original intact church in the Taos area.

As with other churches of its time, St. Francis de Assisi was built in a cruciform shape, measuring 120 feet long. Also, like other churches mentioned in this book, the adobe church has gone through many transformations, with the addition of buttresses, vigas, corbels, flanking bell towers and sanctuary woodwork. O'Keeffe described Rancho de Taos as "one of the most beautiful buildings left in the United States by the early Spaniards." Designated a National Historic Landmark in 1970, it was also given the honor of being named a World Heritage Church as well.

Contained within the church walls is a painting that some consider miraculous—mysterious, to say the least. *The Shadow of the Cross* oil painting depicts Jesus Christ standing on the shore of the Sea of Galilee. In the daylight, it is a beautiful late-nineteenth-century work by French Canadian painter Charles Henry Ault. But when the light is turned off, the mystery beings. Several images appear in the painting, all glowing. A cross appears over the Lord's left shoulder, a fishing boat appears, the eyes always follow the observer and the foot always points to the observer. This painting was created before luminescent paint was developed. Tests have been done on the paint and canvas, but, to date, no one can explain the occurrences.

Rancho de Taos was beloved by artist Georgia O'Keeffe as a favorite subject matter.

St. Joseph Apache Mission, Mescalero

Situated in the Sacramento Mountains, perched on a hill slightly off Highway 70 in Mescalero, New Mexico, is the magnificent St. Joseph Apache Mission Church. Jutting out from the pine trees, the stone structure stretches skyward from Highway 70, beckoning those who pass to stop and reflect. Dedicated to the veterans of World War II, St. Joseph Apache Mission was built through the valiant efforts of Father Arthur Braun, a World War II chaplain and prisoner of war during his military career. After his death in 1983, his remains were returned to Mescalero and buried in the sanctuary.

Built in a cruciform shape, the church is 64 feet wide and 131 feet long and features 50-foot ceilings, 80 feet at the peak. The tip of the cross that adorns the bell tower reaches 103 feet toward heaven, and the bell tower walls are 4 feet thick at the base. The stained-glass windows were installed by a company from El Paso in 1961. Floor tiles were obtained by the nearby La Luz Pottery Plant. The lighting fixtures were brought up from Juarez, Mexico.

Mescalero Apache traditions are also celebrated in St. Joseph's through murals and artwork inside the sanctuary. The Stations of the Cross were imported from the Philippines in honor of Father Braun's service in that

St. Joseph Apache Mission serves the Mescalero Apache Reservation in southeastern New Mexico.

country, where he was held captive. Today, St. Joseph Apache Mission Church is still a vital part of the Mescalero community, providing important services for the parish families. A gift shop offers Native American items for sale and information for visitors. Proceeds go to the continuing preservation of this important church.

Basilica of San Albino, Mesilla

On the north end of the small Mesilla Plaza sits the Basilica of San Albino, one of the oldest missions in the Mesilla Valley and often called the most outstanding edifice of the plaza. The church you see today was constructed in 1906 on top of the foundation of the old adobe church. When Hispanic settlers came to the valley, they developed La Mesilla in 1850, including a central plaza and the Catholic church, which was constructed primitively of mud and logs on the south side of the plaza between 1855 and 1857.

Under the leadership of the bishop from Durango, Mexico, La Mesilla received a papal decree that created the Vicariate Apostolic of New Mexico in 1850. This allowed Padre Bernardino Hinojos to become the first permanent pastor in 1852. With the Gadsden Purchase of 1853–54, La Mesilla was transferred to the New Mexico diocese since large portions of present-day Arizona and New Mexico were added. This diocese was under the direction of Bishop Jean Baptiste Lamy.

In order to protect the church and community from raids, the building was moved to its present location at the north end of the plaza in 1856. Due to Bishop Lamy's disdain for adobe construction, San Albino received a French-European façade in 1857. The first bell for the church was commissioned in 1876 and cast out of copper. Two more bells, named Sagrado Corazon de Jesus and Maria Albina, were cast in 1886. The largest and final bell, named Campaña Grande, was hung in 1887. These bells were christened and given godparents to care for them by tradition and are still used today.

San Albino Church was dedicated in 1908 and declared a minor basilica on November 1, 2008, which was also the Feast of All Saints. When visiting San Albino, please visit the gift shop, which supports the church.

BIBLIOGRAPHY

Books

Baddle, Paul. *Maria of Guadalupe: Shaper of History, Shaper of Hearts*. San Francisco, CA: Ignatius Press, 2009.

Bandelier, Adolph F., and Edgar L. Hewitt. *Indians of the Rio Grande Valley*. Albuquerque: University of New Mexico Press, 1937.

Beck, Warren A. *New Mexico: A History of Four Centuries*. Norman: University of Oklahoma Press, 1963.

Bolton, Herbert Eugene. *Coronado: Knight of Pueblos and Plains*. Albuquerque: University of New Mexico Press, 1949.

———. *Spanish Exploration in the Southwest, 1542–1706*. New York: Charles Scribner's Sons, 1916.

Butcher, Devereux. *Exploring Our Prehistoric Indian Ruins*. Washington, DC: National Parks Association, 1955.

Cash, Marie Romero. *Built of Earth and Song: Churches of Northern New Mexico*. Santa Fe: Museum of New Mexico Press/Red Crane Books, 2008.

Chavez, Fray Angelico. *La Conquistadora: The Autobiography of an Ancient Statue*. Paterson, NJ: St. Anthony Guild Press, 1954.

Churches of New Mexico: The Postcard Archive Series. Santa Fe: Museum of New Mexico Press, 1994.

Cook, Mary J. Straw. *Loretto: The Sisters and Their Santa Fe Chapel*. Santa Fe: Museum of New Mexico Press, 2002.

Crutchfield, James A. *It Happened in New Mexico*. Guilford, CT: Globe Pequot Press, 1995.

Davis, Nancy Yaw. *The Zuni Enigma*. New York: W.W. Norton & Company, 2000.

De Aragon, Ray John. *Hidden History of Spanish New Mexico*. Charleston, SC: The History Press, 2012.

Dominguez, Fray Francisco Atanasio. *The Missions of New Mexico, 1776.* Albuquerque: University of New Mexico Press, 1956.

Drain, Thomas. *A Sense of Mission: Historic Churches of the Southwest.* San Francisco, CA: Chronicle Books, 1994.

Ebright, Malcolm, and Rick Hendricks. *The Witches of Abiquiu: The Governor, the Priest, the Genizaro Indians and the Devil*. Albuquerque: University of New Mexico Press, 2006.

Ebright, Malcolm, Rick Hendricks and Richard W. Hughes. *Four Square Leagues: Pueblo Indian Land in New Mexico.* Albuquerque: University of New Mexico Press, 2015.

Ellis, Bruce T. *Bishop Lamy's Santa Fe Cathedral: With Records of the Old Spanish Church (Parroquia) and Convent Formerly on the Site*. Albuquerque: University of New Mexico Press, 1985.

Emerson, Dorothy. *Among the Mescalero Apaches: The Story of Father Albert Braun, O.F.M.* Tucson: University of Arizona Press, 1973.

Espinosa, J. Manuel. *The Pueblo Indian Revolt of 1696 and the Franciscan Missions in New Mexico*. Norman: University of Oklahoma Press, 1991.

Fedewa, Marilyn H. *Maria of Agreda: Mystical Lady in Blue*. Albuquerque: University of New Mexico Press, 2009.

Folsom, Franklin. *Indian Uprising on the Rio Grande: The Pueblo Revolt of 1680.* Albuquerque: University of New Mexico Press, 1973.

Forrest, Earle R. *Missions and Pueblos of the Old Southwest.* Cleveland, OH: Arthur H. Clark Company, 1929.

Graziano, Frank. *Historic Churches of New Mexico Today*. New York: Oxford University Press, 2019.

Gutierrez, Ramon A. *When Jesus Came, the Corn Mothers Went Away: Marriage, Sexuality, and Power in New Mexico, 1500–1846*. Stanford, CA: Stanford University Press, 1991.

Hall, G. Emlen. *Four Leagues of Pecos: A Legal History of the Pecos Grant, 1800–1933*. Albuquerque: University of New Mexico Press, 1983.

Hall-Quest, Olga Wilbourne. *Conquistadors and Pueblos: The Story of the American Southwest, 1540–1848*. New York: Dutton and Company, 1969.

Hammond, George P., and Agapito Rey. *The Rediscovery of New Mexico, Coronado Cuarto Centennial Publication 1540–1940*. Vol. 111. Albuquerque: University of New Mexico Press, 1966.

Hayes, Aiden C. *The Four Churches of Pecos*. Albuquerque: University of New Mexico Press, 1974.

Hickerson, Nancy Parrott. *The Jumanos, Hunters and Traders of the South Plains*. Austin: University of Texas Press, 1994.

Hughes, Lenore Harris. *Holy Adobe*. El Paso, TX: Hughes Publishing Company, 1981.

Jenkins, Myra Ellen, and Albert Schroeder. *A Brief History of New Mexico*. Albuquerque: University of New Mexico Press, 1974.

Jones, Robert C. *Ghost Towns, Forts and Pueblos of New Mexico*. Kennesaw, GA: self-published, 2014.

Kessell, John L. *Kiva, Cross and Crown: The Pecos Indians and New Mexico 1540–1840*. Washington, DC: National Parks Service, 1979.

———. *The Missions of New Mexico Since 1776*. Santa Fe, NM: Sunstone Press, 2012

———. *Spain in the Southwest, a Narrative History of Colonial New Mexico, Arizona, Texas and California*. Norman: University of Oklahoma Press, 1995.

Kubler, George. *The Religious Architecture of New Mexico: In the Colonial Period and Since the American Occupation*. Albuquerque: Published for the School of American Research by the University of New Mexico Press, 1973.

LeFree, Betty. *Santa Clara Pottery Today*. Albuquerque: University of New Mexico Press, 1975.

Lewis, Brother B. *Oldest Church in the U.S.: Story of the San Miguel of St. Michael's High School*. Santa Fe, NM: San Miguel Church, 1957.

Lummis, Charles. *The Land of Poco Tiempo*. Albuquerque: University of New Mexico Press, 1966.

———. *Mesa, Cañon and Pueblo: Our Wonderland of the Southwest—Its Marvels of Nature—Its Pageant of the Earth Building—Its Strange Peoples—Its Centuried Romance*. New York: Century Company, 1925.

Marmon, Lee. *Laguna Pueblo: A Photographic History*. Albuquerque: University of New Mexico Press, 2015.

Marriott, Alice. *Indians of the Four Corners: The Anasazi and Their Pueblo Descendants*. Santa Fe, NM: Ancient City Press, 1996.

———. *Maria: The Potter of San Ildefonso*. Norman: University of Oklahoma Press, 1976.

Minge, Ward Alan. *Acoma: Pueblo in the Sky*. Albuquerque: University of New Mexico Press, 1976.

Morris, Juddi. *Tending the Fire*. Flagstaff, AZ: Northland Publishing, 1997.

Morrow, Baker H., trans. and ed. *A Harvest of Reluctant Souls: The Memorial of Fray Alonso de Benavides, 1630*. Niwot: University Press of Colorado, 1996.

Murphy, Dan. *Salinas Pueblo Missions: Abo, Quarai and Gran Quivira*. Tucson, AZ: Southwest Parks and Monuments Association, 1993.

Najera, Pedro de Cantañeda. *Narrative of the Coronado Expedition*. Chicago: Lakeside Press, 2002.

Nickens, Paul, and Kathleen Nickens. *Pueblo Indians of New Mexico*. Charleston, SC: Arcadia Publishing, 2008.

Noble, David Grant, ed. *Living the Ancient Southwest*. Santa Fe, NM: School for Advanced Research Press, 2014.

Otero-Warren, Nina. *Old Spain in Our Southwest*. Chicago: Rio Grande Press, 1962.

Pacheco, Ana. *Pueblos of New Mexico*. Charleston, SC: Arcadia Publishing, 2018.

Parsons, Francis B. *Early 17th Century Missions of the Southwest*. Tucson, AZ: Dale Stuart King Publisher, 1975.

Pike, David. *Roadside New Mexico*. Albuquerque: University of New Mexico Press, 2004.

Rakocy, Bill. *Great Western Missions: Exhibition October 4–31, 1987*. El Paso, TX: El Paso Museum of Art, 1987.

Rohn, Authur H. *Pueblo Ruins of the Southwest*. Albuquerque: University of New Mexico Press, 2006.

Sando, Joe S. *The Pueblo Indians*. San Francisco, CA: Indian Historian Press, 1976.

Sandoval, Richard C. *Explore New Mexico: Insider's Guide: Getaways in the Land of Enchantment*. Santa Fe: New Mexico Magazine, 1989.

Sheppard, Carl. *The Archbishop's Cathedral*. Santa Fe, NM: Cimarron Press, 1994.

Simmons, Marc. *New Mexico: An Interpretive History*. Albuquerque: University of New Mexico Press, 1977.

Spicer, Edward. *Cycles of Conquest*. Tucson: University of Arizona Press, 1962.

Stanley, Francis. *The Zia, New Mexico Story*. Pep, TX: self-published, 1969.

Terrell, John Upton. *Pueblos, Gods and Spaniards*. New York: Dial Press, 1973.

Thomas, Alfred B., trans., ed. and anno. *Forgotten Frontiers. A Study of the Spanish Indian Policy of Don Juan Bautista de Anza, Governor of New Mexico, 1777–1787: from the Original Documents in the Archives of Spain, Mexico and New Mexico.* Norman: University of Oklahoma Press, 1932.

Treib, Marc. *Sanctuaries of Spanish New Mexico*. Berkley: University of California Press, 1993.

Twitchell, Ralph E. *Leading Fact in New Mexico History*. Vols. 1 & 2. Cedar Rapids, IA: Torch Press, 1911.

———. *Spanish Archives of New Mexico.* 2 vols. Cedar Rapids, IA: Torch Press, 1914.

Wingert-Playdon, Kate. *John Gaw Meem at Acoma: The Restoration of San Estaban del Rey Mission.* Albuquerque: University of New Mexico Press, 2012.

Wormington, H.M. *Prehistoric Indians of the Southwest.* Denver, CO: Denver Museum of Natural History, 1975.

Articles

Beckworth, Frank. "A Day in Acoma." *El Palacio* 35 (December 1933): 207–8.

Bloom, Lansing B. "Bourke on the Southwest." *New Mexico Historical Review* 8, no. 1 (1933): 6, 8.

Bolton, Herbert E. "The Mission as a Frontier Institution in the Spanish-American Colonies." *American Historical Review* 18, no. 1 (October 1917): 42–61.

Boswell, Alisa. "Zia Pueblo Say They Want Symbol Used Respectfully." *Albuquerque Journal*, April 21, 2015.

Kelly, Henry W. "Franciscan Missions of New Mexico, 1740–1760." *New Mexico Historical Review* 15 (1940): 345–68; 16 (1941): 41–69.

Melzer, Richard. "La Historia Del Rio Abajo. The Curse of Gran Quivira." *Valencia County News-Bulletin*, January 13, 2017.

Scholes, France V. "Documents for the History of the New Mexico Missions in the Seventeenth Century." *New Mexico Historical Review* 4 (1929): 45–48.

Online Sources

New Mexico Nomad. www.newmexiconomad.com.

Mission Websites

Jemez. http://jemezpueblo.com.

Kewa. http://santodomingotribe.org.

Laguna. www.lagunapueblo-nsn.gov.

Nambé. http://nambepueblo.org.

Ohkay Owingeh. http://ohkay.org.

Picuris. www.picurispueblo.org or http://www.laplaza.org/penasco/picuris.
Pojoaque. http://pojoaque.org.
San Ildefonso. www.sanipueblo.org.
Santa Ana. www.santana.org.
Taos. http://taospueblo.com.
Zia. http://zia.com/home/zia_info.html.

INDEX

T

U

V

W

Y

Z

ABOUT THE AUTHOR

Courtesy of Amanda Birchell.

As a New Mexico native, Donna Blake Birchell has always been fascinated with the rich history of her home state. She was introduced to the legends and lore by her father in her childhood. Raised Catholic, she was spiritually drawn to the mission churches as she explored the state, a feeling she wanted to share with others.

Visit us at
www.historypress.com